LOOK AT MY
PEOPLE

BLESSED BY TRIALS,
HEALED BY FAITH

KEVIN M. WARD

WESTBOW
P R E S S®
A DIVISION OF THOMAS NELSON
& ZONDERVAN

WestBow Press books may be ordered through booksellers or by contacting:

WestBow Press
A Division of Thomas Nelson & Zondervan
1663 Liberty Drive
Bloomington, IN 47403
www.westbowpress.com
844-714-3454

Scripture quotations are taken from the New King James Version. Copyright © 1982 by Thomas Nelson, Inc. Used by permission. All rights reserved.

ISBN: 979-8-3850-2697-5 (sc)
ISBN: 979-8-3850-2698-2 (hc)
ISBN: 979-8-3850-2696-8 (e)

Library of Congress Control Number: 2024911521

Print information available on the last page.

WestBow Press rev. date: 06/13/2024

A SPECIAL THANK YOU
AND DEDICATION

I would like to thank my family and my children for being by my side during many difficult times of pain and suffering through out the last couple of decades of my life. Their love and prayers for me gave me the strength to fight and victoriously win through Jesus Christ.

I would like to give a special thanks to my Pastor and Dear friend Pastor James Hogan for not only editing this book but truly being by my side for the last decade. He has witnessed continuous attacks from satan on my life and God has used Hogan to open the deep spiritual life in Jesus that I now live.

I dedicate this book to Judah. Judah was the kindest loving young man that I have ever known. He struggled from mental disabilities as a result from child abuse as a baby before his loving adopted family had rescued him. Judah was the stranger that the bible talks about. He blessed my life at a time when I myself thought my life was over due to my health.

CONTENTS

1. An Introduction 1
2. My Loving Family 6
3. Nearly gone at two.. 10
4. Night terrors 16
5. Superman crashes to Earth............................. 20
6. Bone Marrow Cancer...................................... 22
7. Dreams of destruction 29
8. High School Nights... 34
9. Surrounded by demons................................... 37
10. Dream of the serpent 42
11. Flights of terror 47
12. Kidney failure 52
13. Darkest Days 55
14. Between the Realms 59
15. Fading as the battle rages............................... 62
16. Losing my family 64
17. The Church 71
18. Proverbs, my failing litmus test..................... 75
19. God Begins Illuminating 79
20. Kidney cancer attacks 90
21. The Good News Place..................................... 94

22. Jesus saves my soul................................ 97

23. The devil brings cancer back 106

24. The Demon Named "pain".........................111

25. Billy Graham Ministries and covid vision.........114

26. Kidney failure, covid..............................117

27. The dying stranger...............................121

28. Visions of Hell.................................. 126

29. The devil and his demons......................... 130

30. Abortion.......................................132

31. The Meeting.................................... 138

32. Baby Corpses as a Commodity.....................144

33. The Last Supper Table 147

34. Two thoughts that trouble me.....................151

35. The demonic politician...........................158

36. What are the signs?..............................163

37. The Holy Spirit Saves Me Again...................170

38. Israel Under attack 174

39. The Natural Man 180

40. The Power of Prayer 185

41. Salvation in Christ............................... 190

42. My friend Judah................................195

CHAPTER ONE

AN INTRODUCTION

There I was, sitting in my living room, watching the news on television, a story out of Washington, DC on the Christian Broadcasting Network (CBN), as I often do. And there he was. That now evil man, subjugated and overtaken by the demon I well know.

I receive visions from the Lord. It strikes me still as a bit strange to put that on paper or hear it from my mouth. I didn't grow up with any understanding or belief in such things, yet, there it is.

I hear the powerful voice of God, a voice that commands attention.

This wasn't always so, but thanks to it and the truths He has revealed I understand my life, my history, and His purposes in ways to which I was blind for years.

His voice is strong and rich. Resonant. The powerful voice of authority, always to the point. It instantly blocks out all outside voices or noises and aligns my spirit with the Holy Spirit. When this occurs, He takes my mind immediately elsewhere in place and time, and I become unaware of my physical surroundings or minutely focused on one thing He desires for me to see and understand.

What you are about to read as an account of attacks on my life from when I was an infant to now. It's about loss and losses, victory and glory. It's about what I didn't grasp before, and how that's changed by God's sovereign decision to engage with me on a deeper, stunning spiritual level.

You will see how Jesus Christ came to me, saving my soul from eternal damnation, and how, at a point when my beard is graying and my body is broken, at a time when many would look at me and say "It's done. Hang up your cleats," God has illuminated a new, powerful and fruitful path.

I am older now, in my sixties.

In agreement with many of my doctors, I shouldn't be alive.

My medical history reads like a novel. Medical experts and cannot explain what I have been through or how I have endured such constant sickness. The hospital bills over my life have eclipsed in the millions of dollars.

To give you a glimpse of my health, I was just again released from the hospital. I haven't yet been home. I came straight to the church, where I serve. And write. It has become my habit, my way. The church is where

I need to be. On Earth, it is where I belong, where my heart is.

Health issues, tapped finances, and spiritual attacks will not stop me. I belong to God, fully. I am His, and He is mine. Jesus is my Savior, my source, the Author and Sustainer of my being, my purpose.

I'm no longer on my own journey, but His mission. Through miraculous healings, visions, and dreams that God has blessed me with I hope you, dear reader, will find inspiration and hope, and a desire to grow and know God's power and engagement at another level.

If you find yourself in agreement with today's spiraling culture, you likely may hate me before you're done reading this book. I expect my reputation and life to be obliterated by today's godless society's attacks for saying what I am about to tell and show you. *If* they can do it. I'm believing that God will carry me through the storm yet again.

I am a Christian and I stand in agreement with the Bible, God's word, the truth. From Genesis to Revelation, I embrace it. Where its truths have rubbed my own soiled sensibilities wrong, it is me who submits. God is right and righteous. I strive for that.

You will read of miracles and truths that the Creator of the universe has manifested before me. You will also be warned... God's clock for us here ticks on, but it won't forever, and we need to know the truths that cascade from that reality.

Blessed are those who are persecuted for righteousness' sake, For theirs is the kingdom of heaven.[11] Blessed are you when they revile and persecute you, and say all kinds of evil against you falsely for My sake. [12] Rejoice and be exceedingly glad, for great is your reward in heaven, for so they persecuted the prophets who were before you. ~**Matthew 5: 10-12**

This is my prayer for this book and those who read this book and all are suffering spiritually and/or physically.

Dear Jesus, our Holy Savior. I thank You for giving me the courage to write this book of messages and visions You have commanded recorded, divine gifts of wisdom and knowledge from You, from God my Father, and from Your Holy Spirit. I pray that You lead me through these passages, and that I am accurate with the details of visions and words You have shown and told me.

I pray that you open the hearts of the readers so they may address their own circumstances in these difficult times in preparation of Your arrival and for living life abiding in You, my

Savior Jesus Christ as You fulfill Your promise to abide in us.

By Your power, may this book change many lives for you, Jesus.

In the name of our Savior Jesus Christ, I ask this, Amen.

CHAPTER TWO

MY LOVING FAMILY

I was born into a family of nine children. I had five sisters and three brothers. I am the seventh child. We've been truly blessed in that God provided us with such a loving and supportive family, and God-loving parents, I love my family with all my heart.

With nine kids already, our parents took in five other people in throughout the years. They believed it was their place to open the door for those they could help.

Two of these "new family members" were friends of mine. Their parents were moving away and they needed to finish high school, and did not want to leave our district because it provided many opportunities and a great education. Both were musicians. One has since died. The other is a world class guitar player, performing to this day.

I am a musician, too. I was always active in school with all of the different bands and, likely due to that, I ended up being elected Senior Class President. I never ran for that position, but someone placed my name on the ballot and I won. I was surprised, for sure.

My father was a writer and news editor and my mother, with a house full of children across the age spectrum, was a full-time homemaker. She was also a musician and had attended Duquesne University in Pittsburgh, in the late 1930s and early 1940s as a classical pianist. She played for years as an organist for many of the cathedrals in Pittsburgh.

My father was educated at Notre Dame and studied writing, composition, journalism and English. He served as a pilot and instructor and trainer in the Army Air-corps during World War two. When I was young, my father wrote many funny stories about us nine kids in the paper. My father's side of the family has a long history of writers and editors. It's a creative career, but takes focus. I'm not sure how Mom and Dad managed it with so many kids around.

The love I experienced from my family throughout my life is irreplaceable, amazing. My family has seen some troubles over the years, but we've always been supportive of each other through difficult times.

I wish I could better put into words the power of my family's prayers and the effect of their love for me. With all of the medical issues and complications I've gone through, I know their prayers have kept me going.

I wonder if they actually know that. I sensed their prayers then, and I do to this day.

Growing up with my family with this rich love binding us together is something I truly cherish in life. With life's challenges, I feel bad for folks who don't know the love of a solid, centered family. In the warm glow of my memories, growing up seems often like some decades long summer camp - fun for the whole family.

Our family would vacation at the Outer Banks of North Carolina. We'd all pile into a massive station wagon, and roll down the road packed in like sardines among blankets and luggage. Each year, we would stop at the same roadside market along the way, and the farmer would recognize us, greeting us and chuckling at us all piling out of the wagon.

My father taught me and my other siblings how to fish in the surf, and we would body surf and swim, picnicking on the beach with our coolers and grill. All these years later, we still talk about those days and the great fun we had. It was idyllic.

When I was 5 years old, my oldest brother went off to college. I was shaken, sad that he left. One by one, my sisters and brothers followed suit. It broke my heart that the family would no longer all live together.

I remember how happy I was when we drove to pick my brother up from school. I can still see him in my mind, sitting, playing his guitar and sporting a beard!

When it was my time to head off to Towson and Baltimore Maryland, to the Music Conservatory, it was very hard on me to go, leaving what was left of my family home. It was hard for my mother and father, as the house was becoming quieter and quieter, with only two kids left to man the ship.

I thought of them and their emotions when my own son Parker went off to school in Louisville, Kentucky.

Later in life when I got very ill, those long held bonds we'd made as kids kept my family on the case, as some of my brothers and sisters would come visit me as I spent months hospitalized. Those who lived far away would call often, and come visit me when they were in town.

I am not going to write much about my career. I entered college as a professional musician and was blessed to study and perform with some of the great artists of this time and of the past. After giving up a full-time career in music I entered the Automotive industry and quickly climbed the path to be an executive consultant for big companies.

I was very successful by the world's standards until I became chronically ill. I was forty-eight years old when I began the difficult road of fighting for my life almost daily. The absolute most difficult times were ahead of me.

CHAPTER THREE

NEARLY GONE AT TWO

When I was 2 years old, my parents had a swimming pool installed at our home. We all loved to swim, but with so many kids, paying to send us to the public pool on summer days was prohibitively expensive.

One day I had my life preserver on as I started paddling from the shallow end of the pool to the deep end. No one else was actually in the pool, but I believe there were a couple of my sisters were there watching from the lawn chairs nearby. I know at least one of my sisters was there.

A phone rang, and my sister raced to the phone and I was left alone, presumably meant to be for only a moment.

At the deep end now, I spun back around my life preserver came loose and fell off. No one was there. I was alone, without a floatation device, and I couldn't yet swim.

I was going to drown.

As I drifted down in the water, I was face up, and, oddly, I don't remember being afraid. It was so colorful. The blues and yellows of the pool liner dazzled in the sunshine. I could see the white ball of the sun through the deepening water above my head, as I sank toward the bottom.

Bubbles were bobbing from my mouth. I watched them rise away from my face one after another until there were no more to rise. That is the last I remember.

And the peace of God, which surpasses all understanding, will guard your hearts and minds through Christ Jesus. ~**Philippians 4:7**

For unto us a Child is born, Unto us a Son is given; And the government will be upon His shoulder. And His name will be called Wonderful, Counselor, Mighty God, Everlasting Father, Prince of Peace. [7] Of the increase of His government and peace There will be no end, Upon the throne of David and over His kingdom, To order it and establish it with judgment and justice From that time forward, even forever. The zeal of the LORD of hosts will perform this ~**Isaiah 9:6-7**

And suddenly there was with the angel a multitude of the heavenly host praising God and saying:[14] "Glory to God in the highest, And on earth peace, goodwill toward men!" ~**Luke 2:13-14**

Peace I leave with you, My peace I give to you; not as the world gives do I give toyou. Let not your heart be troubled, neither let it be afraid. ~**John 14:27**

Now may the God of hope fill you with all joy and peace in believing, that you may abound in hope by the power of the Holy Spirit. ~**Romans 15:13**

Years later, I was told that a neighbor from two houses down had been walking near our yard and saw me on the bottom of the pool. He rescued me. If it were not for him, I would have died.

I grew up aware of the incident, sure it was simply a bad moment, a lapse in babysitting attention, and, thankfully, a tragedy averted.

I know better now. Not by assumption or years of retrospective analysis. I know because, for His reasons, God, after many years, showed me.

Fear not, for I am with you; Be not dismayed, for I am your God. I will strengthen you, Yes, I will help you, I will uphold you with My righteous right hand.' ~*Isaiah 41:10*

Let your conduct be without covetousness; be content with such things as you have. For He Himself has said, "I will never leave you nor forsake you." ⁶ So we may boldly say: "The LORD is my helper; I will not fear. What can man do to me?" ~**Hebrews 5:7**

For God has not given us a spirit of fear, but of power and of love and of a sound mind. ~**2 Timothy 1:7**

The LORD is my shepherd; I shall not want. ² He makes me to lie down in green pastures; He leads me beside the still waters. ³ He restores my soul; He leads me in the paths of righteousness For His name's sake. ⁴ Yea, though I walk through the valley of the shadow of death, I will fear no evil; For You are with me; Your rod and Your staff, they comfort me ~**Psalm 23:1-4**

Be strong and of good courage, do not fear nor be afraid of them; for the LORD our God, He is the One who goes with you. He will not leave you nor forsake you." **~Deuteronomy 31:6**

Peace I leave with you, My peace I give to you; not as the world gives do I give to you. Let not your heart be troubled, neither let it be afraid. **~John 14:27**

The LORD is my light and my salvation; Whom shall I fear? The LORD is the strength of my life; Of whom shall I be afraid? **~Psalm 27:1**

God is our refuge and strength, A very present help in trouble. ² Therefore we will not fear, Even though the earth be removed, And though the mountains be carried into the midst of the sea; ³ Though its waters roar and be troubled, Though the mountains shake with its swelling. Selah **~Psalm 46:1-3**

Cast your burden on the LORD, And He shall sustain you; He shall never permit the righteous to be moved ~ **Psalm 55:22**

He who dwells in the secret place of the Most- High Shall abide under the shadow of the Almighty. [2] I will say of the LORD, "He is my refuge and my fortress; My God, in Him I will trust." ~**Psalm 91:1-2**

CHAPTER FOUR

NIGHT TERRORS

When I was four years old I started having bad dreams. True nightmares, really.

At that tender age, I was so afraid. To this day, I can call up the memory of the fear I had at night, and even now, it can bring tears to my eyes. It was so hard on my life as a little boy. To this day, I do not like darkness.

I thank Jesus for my loving parents who would hear me crying and comfort me.

When I was four, in 1964, I slept on the bottom bunk bed in the room I shared with my older brother.

Our family was like the old Waltons TV show at bedtime. We would always call out, 'Night Mom, Night Dad, love you, have a nice sleep and dream. We would all say it to each other. It gave me so much comfort and the feeling of love from my family. When the conversation died off, we'd pray silently, each in our own bed, and drift off to sleep.

For me, then the dreams started.

In the first of these ugly dreams, I was in my parent's basement. I knew our cellar quite well, for I would often go down there with my stretchy rubber Pokie and Gumby action figures, from the old Gumby television show, and play with them on the linoleum floor. More often than not, my mother was also down there, doing laundry for all of us - a never-ending chore in a house that full of people.

We had a white washing machine with big rollers on it to wring the water from the clothes. The machine amazed me, but it was off limits - those rollers could catch a four-year-old's hand in no time, so Mom made it clear I was not to touch the machine.

The floor in the basement had a pattern of cream and soft red colored squares. The steps from upstairs were in the corner of the room, across from the laundry, and they were painted gray.

In the dream, I was in the basement facing the steps from the other end of the room. My brothers and sisters were at the bottom of the step. There were smooth, white figures standing with them. They had big, beautiful wings, and their skin glowed. I knew these were angels.

The angels were tall. Much taller than all my family, but I didn't feel afraid. I could tell these were serious beings, but they weren't threatening in any manner. We'd heard of "guardian angels" in church, and I figured this must be the ones assigned to protect our family.

Suddenly, with a collective gasp, my brothers, sisters

and the angels all turned toward me with fear in their eyes, and all of them started running up the steps away from me. I was startled and afraid, but didn't know why they had run. In total panic, I ran for the steps after my family.

As I ran, big black wings encircled me and would not let me run. The wings covered all but my head and I could see my terrified family running up the steps away from me.

I was crying and screaming so hard. My feet would move but I could not get away. I could see them, and the wings, but not the face of the monster who'd snagged me. I cried and cried by myself!

My parents heard me cry and came charging down the stairs from their bedroom to comfort me.

I remember telling my parents that I was afraid of the devil monster. That was all I could say as a 4-year-old.

They got me calmed down, but when they returned to their bedroom, I was so frightened I hid under my covers and cried myself to sleep.

But this was just the beginning. The dreams would occur over and over.

Thus began a cycle where these nightly horror shows would occur, and I would wake up terrified. Then, eventually, I would cry myself to sleep out of exhaustion, and sleep as long as there were no dreams.

These dreams, horrid, terrifying variations of the first dream, would occur several times a week and sometimes every night.

Sometimes the devil monster would let me run all the way to the top, then his big black wings would come crushing in around me and drag me down the steps with his claw-like hands, never allowing me to make my escape upstairs.

In the odd way of dreams, sometimes the stairs would appear straight without their landing and no turn, leaving me a hellishly long climb toward the top. Even with the slight chance in architecture the dream would play out the same way. My family and the angels flee in fear, I try, only to be swooped up yet again, trapped.

Time passed, and the dreams morphed and progressed.

In one recurring version, the devil monster would drag me up to the top step and drag me down the steps over and over, banging me off the stairs. It seemed so real every time, frightening to think about to this day.

I would cry all night until my parents would come to comfort me. The scars to my psyche are real. I don't like sleeping at night in the dark to this day.

The dreams would change as I got older, becoming more violent towards me, and even more frightening.

Throughout, I thought surely other kids had an overactive imagination that brought out nightmares while they tried to rest. The dreams were very realistic, but they're just dreams, right?

CHAPTER FIVE

SUPERMAN CRASHES TO EARTH

One day, while I was in kindergarten, my oldest brother picked the rest of us up from school in the parent's station wagon. Seven of us crammed into the car, the station wagon packed with Ward children.

I locked the door as we all always did, but as the car rounded a bend, the door flew open, and I flew out of the car. My siblings said I looked like Superman with my arms extended ahead of me as I crash landed onto a sidewalk. My leg slammed on the curb's edge.

I had a broken leg and was pretty scuffed up. Certainly, just a case of a young driver not ensuring everyone was safely in the car, and a kindergartner who failed to properly push down the long door lock post, right? A broken leg and lucky to be just that.

When I was 11 years-old a new nightmare began at night.

These were exhausting, horribly frightening, violent and pure evil. My developing mind seemingly could manifest much more gore and ugliness as I climbed the ladder of years. The snatch and grab of the old dreams was positively tame by comparison. Now, each night was a killing floor of gruesome butchery.

For four years these scenes consistently troubled me. My nights were brutal, and I operated on very little rest, making functioning extremely difficult for me during the days. I couldn't fall asleep from fear of what awaited me in the dream world, and I was exhausted.

The dreams were always on my mind. I wished I could just go without sleep. I kept the dreams to myself, other than talking to my mother a couple of times about it, knowing she would always love and comfort me. Later, I refused to even tell her about the dreams because I could tell she was worried about me.

I was on my own and so very afraid of sleeping.

As the 1960s arrived, our family moved to the countryside. It was perfect for our large family - big houses, with big yards surrounded by neighbors that had big families like ours. It was a great place to live. I still went without much sleep for years, but the environs were nicer.

CHAPTER SIX

BONE MARROW CANCER

During the Summer following 8th grade, I became very ill. Lymph nodes were swollen all over my body, and testing discovered my white blood cell count was high, while my red blood count was low.

I ran fevers all the time and sometimes it was hard to swallow because the lymph nodes in my throat were swollen.

I was sent to a children's hospital department at a hospital far from home, recommended to my parents by my uncle. There, I missed my family tremendously. I was 12 and, in that era, there was no room in the hospital for adults. It was set up like an infirmary one might see in an old movie.

I was put in a room surrounded by dozens of sick children and babies fighting, some dying, of cancer.

The children would cry for their parents every night. It broke my heart and I would talk to them and tell the little one's stories. They would calm down for a while, but the crying was never far off.

At that time in my life, I'd started studying drums and music and I was already performing music, so I would sing to the children and try to have them sing along. Most of the children would join in, but some couldn't.

Some were too sick. Others were too committed to crying for their folks, living out an endless lonely tantrum as they missed their people. My heart broke for them and I would spend time praying for them at night.

After thinking hard about how to help these children, I came up with an idea. I asked my mom and dad to bring my harmonica.

They did and I started drawing the kids into a nightly sing-along while I played the harmonica. All of the children were singing and smiling, and it seemed my concern, my prayers, and my efforts were rewarded in a manner that I cherish to this day. That first night, all of the children fell asleep without crying!

My mother and father visited me every night and I could see the sadness in their eyes. The redness in and around their eyes made it obvious that they were shedding many tears about my circumstance.

I worried about my family. I wasn't very much afraid or concerned about me, but I was troubled by the sadness in my parents' eyes. It broke my heart then, and still does as I am writing this today.

I pray for those children I knew in the hospital, that those who survived the scourge of cancer went on to have a loving, healthy life… and that those whose cancer battle was lost won the victory of finding themselves in the arms of Jesus.

In the hospital, I went through countless tests and had several lymph nodes removed from my neck. The tests were unbearably painful. Bone marrow tests on my hips were the worst. The procedure was torture!

The staff laid me on my side on a gurney, and strapped my head shut with a towel in my mouth to prevent me from swallowing my tongue. Then they strapped my body with belts to the gurney and had nurses holding me down.

The doctor pulled out a big hollow needle. It was more like a rod. It was about 10 inches long and it had a gear-like piece situated above the point. It had a handle on the end for the doctor to hold on to.

They administered local anesthetic, then the doctor took the rod-like needle and literally hammered it into my right hip. It was by far the worst pain I'd ever felt. I was screaming and couldn't move. The rod broke my hip, and they started draining the marrow out of the bone into a vial. It was torture! After draining the marrow, the doctor used the gear-like end to chip and bring out part of the bone.

I could not take the pain and I had no way to avoid it, nowhere to go. It was unbelievably excruciating. I was strapped down with my mouth strapped shut, yet I could not stop screaming! The brutality continued for almost an hour.

When the ghastly maneuver finally ended, they kept me strapped to the gurney and said they had needed to test the samples.

They came back 15 minutes later. Cancer.

As bad as that news sounded, I liked what they said next even less.

They had to do the same procedure on my left hip! I remember begging the doctors not to do it again.

"No! I can't do it! I can't take the pain; it will kill me!" I screamed.

The doctors knew I was extremely home sick and how I loved my family. They told me I could go home for the weekend if I completed the test. I cried and pleaded again with them. I always knew what the doctors were doing, why they were doing different tests and procedures, and, I think because my folks always told me what was happening and why, the doctors never held anything back to me even as a kid.

I knew I had no choice and I suffered the intrusion on my left hip as I had on my right hip. It was even worse because of anticipation. On the right hip, I didn't know exactly how it would feel. Now, I knew each step and each screaming, jutting pain. How the pain would start sharp and bright, and only swell and blossom from there as they went through the procedure. They helped me turn over, and strapped me down, strapping my mouth closed again. The whole shebang. Punching through my hip again, draining the marrow. Chipping the hip bone and dragging the chip out. It was terrible.

They let me go home that weekend as promised. It felt so good to see my family. I was home. Even so, I worried about the sick babies back at the hospital.

After the weekend, I arrived back at the hospital for more tests. My lymph nodes were swollen around my neck and under my arms again. The doctors removed more lymph nodes. The doctors knew this was going to be a treacherous road for me, and were kind and concerned as they treated me, running tests and talking about different approaches they might try to address the cancer concerns.

I kept praying for the children. My family kept praying for me.

The next week my lymph node swelling seemed to settle. Tests were run and the doctors were astounded to find my white blood count lowered within normal range, while my red blood count was high, showing that my marrow had started doing its job again.

More tests were run. No signs of cancer. My prayers had been answered! Jesus healed me!

After I was released from the hospital and went back to school, my neck was wrapped with bandages and I was certainly well-bruised and beat up. My school friends told me they had thought I had died. That was a shock to hear.

Of course, that could've come true. I mean, cancer is like the world's ugliest lottery... some unfortunate folks just have the unlucky number come up for them, and some of them don't make it. Nothing nefarious, there, right? Just luck-of-the-draw.

The LORD will strengthen him on his bed of illness; You will sustain him on his sickbed. ~**Psalm 41:3**

Is anyone among you sick? Let him call for the elders of the church, and let them pray over him, anointing him with oil in the name of the Lord. ~**James 5:14**

And heal the sick there, and say to them, 'The kingdom of God has come near to you. ~**Luke 10:9**

O LORD my God, I cried out to You, And You healed me. ~**Psalm 30:2**

He sent His word and healed them, And delivered them from their destructions. ~**Psalm 107:20**

Be strong and of good courage, do not fear nor be afraid of them; for the LORD your God, He is the One who goes with you. He will not leave you nor forsake you. ~ **Deuteronomy 31:6**

O Lord, by these things men live; And in all these things is the life of my spirit; So You will restore me and make me live. [17] Indeed it was for my own peace That I had great bitterness; But You have lovingly delivered my soul from the pit of corruption, For You have cast all my sins behind Your back. ~**Isaiah 38:16-17**

But when Jesus heard it, He answered him, saying, "Do not be afraid; only believe, and she will be made well." ~**Luke 8:50**

CHAPTER SEVEN

DREAMS OF DESTRUCTION

Having such intense and horrifying nightmares for so many years, from such a young age, I wondered if many kids suffered so at night. I wondered if I just had a nasty imagination that brought out all of my subconscious fear when my mind tried to shut down for the night.

I also, if I'm being honest, wondered if these crazy, violent dreams were more than just dreams. Some message perhaps? Some harbinger of ugliness to come? I can't say I thought they were in some way, perhaps, real. But they were so terrifying and vivid in their gruesome gore and terror, that they felt real enough when my mind was conjuring them in the wee hours of the night.

Another new group of nightmares began as elementary school was wrapping up.

I would fall asleep at night, then gentle thoughts I had intentionally held in my mind as I started to drift off would turn into destructive and desolate, torturous messes that terrified me.

I'd find myself the only person left on Earth and an army of demon soldiers, reminiscent of the old Nazi SS, were hunting for me.

The entire landscape was destroyed from war. Destruction reigned in the apocalyptic, barren waste. Shattered buildings, piles of brick and concrete, and jagged torn metal as far as I could see. I remember seeing pictures of Dresden, Germany in the aftermath of weeks of Allied bombing during WWII, and this landscape harkened back to those scenes.

It was always dark, the ground wet and treacherously littered with debris. A swallowing, thick gloominess made seeing difficult. The only lights were sweeping search lights looking for me.

There were no real colors left in the world. The doom-laden blackness only turned a dark gray when the light swept in, concrete dust covering everything. It was always night.

In my dreams, it was as if I were a Jew during the days following Cristallnacht, the 1938 night that launched what would become the Holocaust, and I was the last one left on Earth. The Nazi demons who wanted me dead. They'd search as I ran or hid, and I could hear them tossing debris as they dug into possible hiding places. I could hear their stomping boots as they moved from one place to another. They never talked, ever. Not to each other, not yelling as they coordinated their efforts, not even shouting for me.

The searchlights swept back and forth, reaching into the night. A dark, soupy fog laid in low-lying areas, making those places even murkier.

Sometimes the demon-Nazis must have thought they spotted something. Then, a bigger, more powerful spotlight would light up areas with an intense brilliance. I always found myself hiding at some point inside one piece of torn metal. The twisted structure was huge and bent, almost like a teepee. It was gray and dark black, part of a larger structure obviously blown apart in some earlier conflagration.

A sharp, jagged tear in the metal provided a gap I could slip through to hide within. It was freezing cold inside. So cold I had to exhale into my shirt and jacket so the Nazi's wouldn't see my breath.

The Nazis were always on my tail. As I moved about, I would run at the right time, timing my movements, so I would not be caught in the searchlight. When I couldn't get to the teepee-like structure, I would dive into some debris. It was always dripping wet and cold, and I shivered, sure the hunters would hear my teeth chattering.

Stealth was difficult as the metal scattered all around made noise every time my foot brushed it. I was terrified! I would hear them getting closer, peek through a crack in the metal, and see them getting closer and closer to me. The boots clacking on the street and clanging on the sheet metal everywhere had me convinced they were right on top of me, making it sound like there was no way to get away from the demons.

The mute demons had shiny silver faces with blood vessels bulging out all over, their square jaws muscular and set with cold, emotionless determination. They had one mission, death for me.

The demons wore draping rain gear and carried short submachine guns and rifles. Their prominent noses, like their jaws and cheeks, were crisscrossed with bulging veins, a terrain map of ridges and valleys.

These Nazi demons, with their cold focus, emanated a sense of evil, darkness, sin, death. The dreams always ended up the same way. After my running and hiding all night, they'd stand next to the torn-up metal I hid within, so close to me I could see their boots and hear them breathe.

Terrified, I would pop awake soaked in sweat, emotionally beat up, tired, exhausted. I struggled every day with a sense of simmering terror. The dreams were always in the back of my mind, reminding me all of the time of the torture I was suffering in my sleep.

The dreams, after all this time, seemed like they would never stop.

I remember telling my mom once what I was dealing with, and she comforted me, which was nice. But she seemed too worried afterward for me to bear, so I stopped sharing,

I felt so alone inside. I hated sleeping. I was exhausted

and afraid all the time, carrying this horrific burden. I was a lot older than when my first series of nightmares started, but I was still a kid.

None of this made any sense to me. I did not know what to do. I often cried myself to sleep, trying to avoid it altogether until exhaustion would overtake me. These Nazi demon dreams finally stopped at the beginning of 9th grade.

Now, there were new dreams.

CHAPTER EIGHT

HIGH SCHOOL NIGHTS

Once the Nazi dreams had ended, a new set of dreams occurred several times a week. These were worse.

So much so, that I'd wake up gasping, out of breath and shaking, covered in sweat, crying in the small hours of the night, shivering. As the sun approached the horizon I'd shake in the shower, still amped up on fear as I'd get ready for school.

As soon as I'd fall asleep, the black wings from the dreams of my earliest years, sporting long, bony fingers and four-inch claw like nails, would grab me again from behind.

The city landscape surrounded me. Tall skyscrapers rose endlessly, and I could hear horns and large vehicles rumbling about. The devil, having grabbed me, would drag me up steps to the roof of a skyscraper. The stairs were gray steel climbing between faded yellow walls. At least 100 flights of stairs. From landing to landing, my head and body banged off steps, walls, and the handrail, as he dragged me all of the way to the roof.

His powerful, weathered hands were monstrous, with vessels protruding from them as around big as the fingers themselves. Knifelike fingernails, black and sharp as razors, topped the end of each finger.

He always grabbed me from behind, dragging me face down, so I could never see his face.

These same black wings from my earliest memories! It was the devil himself, again!

By the time he stepped onto the roof, I couldn't do anything. I was beaten, bruised and bleeding. Barely conscious, I could hardly stand.

This roof was higher than all the others, hovering above roofs of the other buildings. I screamed as the devil's black wings dragged me to the edge of the skyscraper, and threw me off into the abyss.

The building was glass and I could see myself falling in the reflections of the glass, floor after floor after floor flashed by as I accelerated toward the ground, screaming the whole way.

Just as the ground approached at terminal speed, I'd wake up.

Exhaustion was my existence. The dream occurred over and over again, all the way through high school. I was sad, lost, and afraid. Physically sore after these ugly dreams, and emotionally battered from the night trauma, it felt as if I had literally experienced a dream event.

I was afraid to tell anyone for what they might think.

I was troubled, but not crazy, and, in those days, getting a reputation for being addled or "touched" was a stigma I could do without. I was already dealing with enough. I had no one to talk to about this. I was on my own.

I remained terrified to fall asleep at night for all four years of high school, wishing the mental torture would end.

CHAPTER NINE

SURROUNDED BY DEMONS

I did have many friends. I must've suffered the lack of sleep with the resilience of a young person, because I did well in school and got along well socially.

One of my best friends lived down the street. Southwestern Pennsylvania, where rivers have cut valleys through the hills, "down the street" often really means down, and it did in this case.

I would ease downslope to visit my friend, and have a great time visiting and goofing off, listening to the latest music and talking about the usual high school mess.

At night, walking home from his house, I would start getting attacked by demons as I climbed back up the hill to my house. Was this my overactive imagination, some trick of the trees and hills and street's shadows, or something different altogether? I didn't know, but it felt real, and was enough to terrify me and hasten the quarter mile climb back up to the house.

The street was very steep, and every time I started to walk, dark black figures would surround me, swirling around me as if they had no need for their feet to touch the ground. Behind the trees and bushes lining the road, I could see more demons dashing back and forth, keeping pace as I went. I tried to be bold and brave, ignoring them, but my courage would always break as I convinced myself that I didn't want to end up in their clutches. I would close my eyes and run, stumbling, sometimes falling.

I would push my body to the limit, running like I'd never run before to get away from them. I'd arrive at home winded, and sometimes scraped up.

Often, my family was in the living room when I came through the door, and I'd be gasping for air, so I would tell my family, I had run up the hill for exercise.

They didn't know I was scared to death. I had struggled with these attacks since I was a baby and now, as a teenager, the attacks were worse. Literally worse, not just qualitatively so. Because this wasn't a nightmare. I was awake, not sleeping, not dreaming. These demons were attacking me when I was wide awake!

Was this just my lot in life? An overly dark, overactive imagination that wouldn't allow me peace asleep or awake? God, I hoped not!

At night, as I slept, the devil snagged and dragged me to toss me from rooftops in my dreams, and, now, during my waking hours, when they would catch me alone, demons would harass and terrify me as I traveled about.

I graduated high school. My early music studies and performances experience paid off and I was accepted in college, studying music. I was so blessed at the music conservatory as I studied and performed with such great young talent from around the country, and got to learn from legends and sit in with them on gigs.

The dreams that had troubled me lessened in frequency while I was at college, and it seemed that real freedom from the torture might truly be at hand. In the short-term, this proved to be true. The dreams finally stopped.

In retrospect, today I am sure it was because of the wild college lifestyle I was living; I was sinning and I now know because of my sin, I was fulfilling the devil's wishes.

The old saying is that the devil doesn't bother putting hurdles in your path if that path leads to perdition.

My lifestyle was about music, but along with that came partying and premarital sex. I was on the wrong path, straying away from God's ways and living in sin.

I finished college, and started performing and traveling around the country sides of America. I often played 6 shows a week in multiple towns, and my lifestyle of sin was becoming my identity. On stage most nights, enjoying the adoration and spotlight, feeding my pride and ego, I was enchanted. After the gigs, we would party late into the night.

No more dreams, I was free from that torture, really for the first time in my life. But my life was all about me, and fame, pride, partying.

I was still very unaware of what was actually going on around and inside of me spiritually. Perhaps if I'd looked at all I'd already been through, I would have seen the fingerprints, the clues of how all these troubles stacked up and the picture they painted. Of how, as I walked, eyes open into a lifestyle of sin, the harassing dreams and inability to rest went away.

But I didn't have any understanding. I just thought my vivid, troubled imagination was tempered by the alcohol and late nights, forcing my mind to shut down as daylight approached and allowing me the first good sleep in years.

I also had no idea of how much I'd forgotten, how many things I couldn't have drawn to mind to examine if I wanted to. It would take God walking me back through the memories of my life to show me the whole picture and the battle that rages around me in the spiritual realm.

Life went on, me oblivious. Later things became very difficult and the attacks became real, not dreams but my physical reality. When I finally turned back to Christ, I learned to understand and be sustained. My faith in Jesus Christ has saved me to this day.

The LORD *is* my light and my salvation; Whom shall I fear? The LORD *is* the strength of my life; Of whom shall I be afraid? **~Psalm 27-1**

Whenever I am afraid, I will trust in You.⁴ In God (I will praise His word), In God I have put my trust; I will not fear. What can flesh do to me? **~Psalm 56:3-4**

Yea, though I walk through the valley of the shadow of death, I will fear no evil; For You *are* with me; Your rod and Your staff, they comfort me. **~Psalm 23:4**

Fear not, for I *am* with you; Be not dismayed, for I *am* your God. I will strengthen you, Yes, I will help you, I will uphold you with My righteous right hand. **~Isaiah 41:10**

Trust in the LORD with all your heart, And lean not on your own understanding; ⁶ In all your ways acknowledge Him, And He shall direct your paths. **~Proverbs 3:5-6**

CHAPTER TEN

DREAM OF THE SERPENT

I performed music almost every night for years. Eventually I burned out from travel, late nights, and partying to the point I was exhausted, and, although I wasn't dreaming much, I'd started to have trouble sleeping again.

In my mid-twenties, I visited my doctor and had me admitted to the hospital for testing. One upside was that I really needed the rest. I had pushed too hard and was paying for it.

Christmas week I spent in the hospital.

This was always a great family get-together time for us, yet Christmas Eve arrived and I was laying in a hospital bed, sad that I wasn't with my family for Christmas. I watched Christmas specials on TV, fell asleep, very troubled. I slept. And dreamt.

In this dream, I stood once again in my parents' basement, next to the fireplace. Suddenly a huge snake appeared, coiled up in front of me. Its head was the size of mine and its body was many, many feet long.

The snake's skin was tan and yellow and its eyes were cold, beady, and red. Somehow I knew this serpent, like the one who'd tempted Adam and Eve in the bible, represented the devil.

The serpent slowly rose up from his coil, waving a few inches side-to-side, until his head was a foot from mine. For the first time ever in a dream, I fought back. I leaned back and punched the snake right in the snout, with all the strength I could muster, and he fell flat to the floor. I hopped forward and began trampling him. I stomped and stomped until the beast was dead!

I woke up winded, yet exhilarated from the tremendous battle in my dream. Exhausted, but victorious. It had been a long season of insomnia capped with short dreamless sleep when my fried mind finally allowed me to doze off.

Now, in the hospital, my first nightmare in years, and - likely tired from being tired and aggravated to have real rest intruded upon - I'd lashed back at the mental attack and gained a victory.

"The LORD is my rock and my fortress and my deliverer; [3] The God of my strength, in whom I will trust; My shield and the horn of my salvation, My stronghold and my refuge; My Savior, You save me from

violence. ⁴I will call upon the LORD, *who
is worthy* to be praised; So shall I be saved
from my enemies. ⁵ "When the waves
of death surrounded me, The floods
of ungodliness made me afraid. ⁶ The
sorrows of Sheol surrounded me; The
snares of death confronted me. ⁷ In my
distress I called upon the LORD, And cried
out to my God; He heard my voice from
His temple, And my cry *entered* His ears.
~ **2 Samuel 22:2-7**

Life went on, and I played music full time for many
years. I fell in love and married at 25, and we had a
beautiful, loving daughter, Lauren, and she took my
heart then and still has it today.

Lauren and I are very much alike.

I remember my sweetie dancing every night and
putting on a show for me, a rhythmic performer like her
drummer father. My little princess, I called her my little
birdie. My wife would stay at her mother's house until I
got home late at night and we'd have dinner there.

Afterward, we would go home. Over time my wife
would go upstairs when we got home, while I'd spend
time with Lauren downstairs. Sadly, I didn't see what
was happening.

We grew apart quickly, barely interacting. She'd
met someone else and before long, I came home and

my wife and Lauren, and their belongings were gone. Soon enough, we divorced. I couldn't understand this but it crushed my heart.

My wife and her new future husband moved to New Jersey to take over a family business and took my daughter away from me, restricting my access to my child. I didn't understand this.

I remember the last day with my daughter as they prepared to leave for Jersey. We celebrated her birthday and she was dressed in a white and black dress. I would go inside the house to cry, not wanting to make Lauren sad on her big day, then come back out, just knowing that my precious 5 year-old was being taken from me.

It was so painful; After they left, I would cry every night for my daughter.

I stayed in touch with my daughter as much as my traveling for work would allow, and would visit when I was able. The pain from the separation from my daughter hurt me so. For years, I really could not celebrate holidays knowing that she was forced by circumstance to be away from me.

My heart was shattered for years, but Lauren and I have a great relationship now that she's an adult. Today, all these years later, I visit my daughter, my loving son in-law and my awesome two grandsons. Praise the Lord!

After the divorce, I stepped back from the music industry completely, and became active in retail automotive sales and automotive business management. After a few years of management, I was offered an automotive training and consulting position that required 11 months of the year traveling around North America. I accepted the position and never turned back.

My business career was lucrative, but required constant travel, leaving me home for roughly a month total per year for many years, consulting for large automotive corporations.

It was very hard on me. The travel schedule was extremely taxing, the job high pressure. There were always deadlines, contracts and objectives to achieve and I never seemed to have time at home.

My priorities were out of whack, and I was too busy to even think about it. As I flew all over North America, I was too swamped to take note that, in many ways, I was drowning in the very swamp affording me a lifestyle of material riches - making me emptier and emptier even as I gathered nice stuff.

CHAPTER ELEVEN

FLIGHTS OF TERROR

One of the flights I flew twice a week was United flight 427 from Pittsburgh to Chicago then back to Pittsburgh, a daily business commuter filled with faces I'd grown familiar with over dozens of turnarounds.

I'd chatted with many of the passengers in the lounge and at the gate, time and again. There were many Mellon Bank employees on every flight, as Mellon was doing lots of development in Illinois then.

One Sunday, in early September of 1994, my flight was booked for the next day's jaunt, but, visiting my mom and dad I noted that they, older now, were having some real health issues. I became very concerned for them as I visited, and, convicted that I must, I canceled the flight and took the week to help my folks.

The flight back to Pittsburgh on Thursday evening, which would have been the return leg for me, crashed due to a rudder malfunction just west of Pittsburgh in

47

a wooded area near Hopewell Township, PA. There were no survivors.

A lot of folks I was friendly with were on that flight, and I remember staring at the television as the local news reported from the debris field, horrified and saddened.

I know Jesus Christ saved me from that flight. It saddens me to this day remembering those people who didn't make it. I praise God for protecting me.

Sometime later, I was in a twelve-passenger twin engine prop plane with a handful of folks while tornadoes were touching down in the outskirts of Pittsburgh.

Airborne, we hit violent turbulence. An alarm rang out, screaming from the cockpit. We had leveled off high above the normal cloud ceiling, but storm tops surrounded us. We could see the tops of the spinning storms rotating and debris churning up from the suction vortices below as the plan shook, tossed to and fro.

It was a short, lightly booked flight on a small plane, with only four passengers and two pilots. In the churning atmosphere, the plane nose- dived. We were going straight down so fast that items in the plane were floating, because of zero gravity, then pinned to the rear of the cabin's ceiling.

The plane shook violently. In those days, prior to 9/11, there was only a drape in that small plane to keep us separated from the cockpit, and it was flat against the ceiling.

The noises you hear in movies, the screaming alarms and whining engines are true - as are the "mayday" calls from the terrified pilots. It was extremely loud and everyone was screaming and crying, terrified.

The co-pilot wedged himself through the cabin door to get eyes on the engines. His eyes confirmed what the cockpit alarm had told him... the left engine was aflame!

"Shut down engine two!" He called over his shoulder to the captain.

The pilot immediately shut down the engine. The shaking and the loud engine noise stopped as we kept losing altitude before we finally felt gravity shift as we leveled off at about one thousand feet.

When we landed the fire department, rescue teams, police and the FAA were there ready for the emergency. We skidded off into the grass at the small airport, dragged by the thrust of one engine, but we made it!

Shaken up, I made my way down the stairs to the ground. I was shocked to see the left propeller split in half. We'd been struck by lightning, and perhaps some ground-based debris thrown into the air by the storm. Thank you, God my Father, for saving us!

I was getting pretty concerned about flying, but the demands of the job didn't subside.

Shortly after that flight, I was on a flight from Philadelphia to Pittsburgh. We took off and the first bell chimed, signaling the plane passing the ten thousand feet mark. Just as it sounded, the pilot hit the intercom button - I assumed he'd only meant the two-way, but got the cabin as well in his panic. I could hear an alarm sounding, high-pitched over the speaker.

"Hard, left!" he barked at the first officer, who had the controls. Then, "Turn right! The huge plane, a Boeing 757, swooped sideways and the pilot screamed "I see Him!" as a corporate jet just missed our left wing. Radar alerts had clued them in, but until that moment, they'd been blind to the other craft's location visually.

When the flight was over, the pilot apologized for hitting the intercom but it was a dire emergency. The co-pilot then explained what had happened and we all cheered and thanked him as we left the aircraft.

That was really close! Jesus saved me and the people again. I have had many close calls while flying but my faith in Jesus Christ as my protector was there for me.

If I had a chance to re-do my career, I would have chosen not to travel. It destroys families, taxes one's health and always made me long for my family.

By no means was money the answer. Sure, I had toys and a large bank account, but I also had a deep sad feeling of being displaced, homeless and lonely. Hotels can't replace home.

I often wondered if the Lord would call me and it's my time to go home to Him, if I'd be found in a hotel room. It was where I laid my lonely head 11 months' worth of each year during that time. Sad.

I continued my consulting career. One day as I was holding a seminar, I met the girl of my dreams. The lady of my dreams, beautiful and so nice and friendly. She was 9 years younger than me and we began dating. Before long, we married. It was a wonderful marriage, although I was traveling. I couldn't wait to come home and see my bride.

We were doing really well together, and built a new house for our home, and life felt great - even though I wished I could stay home more. God gave us a son, Parker, who has been an amazing blessing since the day he arrived on the scene.

I missed my family while I worked, but I was in a good place mentally and spiritually. No bad dreams, no attacks on me from the devil. I remember my son and my wife waving goodbye to me when I headed out of town for work.

I will never forget the terrible sad feeling I had when I was leaving. It was such a blessing to have them, yet our bills were paid by my career and the travels it entailed.

I never told my wife much about how I felt about that. I knew it was my responsibility to provide and maintain the lifestyle they were accustomed to regardless how weary and lonely I felt missing my wife and son on the road. My father did what it took to provide for his family when we were growing up, even the parts he didn't enjoy. I would do the same.

CHAPTER TWELVE

KIDNEY FAILURE

When our son was a baby, I was traveling, in Chicago. After a long day of hustling about, my feet hurt. When I took off my shoes, I noticed my feet were badly swollen.

I've never been overweight, and am not now, but one wouldn't have known that by seeing my feet then. They swelled to the point where I could not tie my shoes. I went to see a doctor. Sadly, it signaled the beginning of a kidney disease that almost killed me then, one I deal with to this day.

I became extremely ill. The doctors had to treat this disease with chemotherapy and steroids, on and off for a year. I could gain dozens of pounds in a day and lose it the next as my malfunctioning kidneys would hoard then release fluid.

It was so painful; My doctors were not sure I was going to make it. At times, neither was I.

I had to stay home in western Pennsylvania and couldn't work. The longing I had to be with my family had been provided, but not by a circumstance that I would've wished upon anyone.

It was a blessing that I was with my son every day. In the time since, as I've grown closer to God and really learned how to focus on Him and hear from Him. I thought the illness was just another luck-of-the-draw thing, one of the things that happens to somebody, and I was the one. Later, when God walked me back through my life, bringing up things long forgotten and showing me behind the spiritual curtain, I learned better.

Little did I know at the time that this was the beginning of the physical issues that would stack up and spiral out of control for me, affecting my body, my livelihood, and my mind in negative ways. I would spend years worth of time hospitalized in the years to come.

I was able to return to work after a year and I was back to the non-stop drain-the-life-out-of-you traveling career.

My doctors, trying to get ahead of my health with some preventative measures, recommended a bone density bisphosphonate drug. The drug was approved and advertised with no side effects.

Designed to strengthen bones and keep them strong, my doctor felt with the amount of traveling I was doing it would keep me sturdy. Ironically, and now tragically so, I had no bone issues or concerns at that time. He was concerned due to my kidney situation, and the sedentary time on planes, followed by zooming from site to site in far away cities to do my job.

I'd finally had too much of traveling and decided to take a job at a local business. I hadn't felt good for a while, but I needed to provide for my family. Cutting out the extraneous travel seemed a good route to go.

We built a newer home and things were going well, but, having met while I was busy traveling, it proved difficult for me, and likely for my wife, to adjust to me being at home more.

I had been independently traveling for over 20 years, and she'd been running a household without much of me around for a good while now.

CHAPTER THIRTEEN

DARKEST DAYS

I remained local, yet my health began to deteriorate rapidly. The medicine meant to strengthen my bones collapsed the arteries in my jaw, my hips and my shoulders.

My bones would spontaneously grow in spots, even coming out through my gums at times. The newly grown bone would die and I would have to have it surgically sawed off. If it was a small, protruding piece, it was so dead and brittle, I could, and did, break it off with my fingers.

The cascade of issues sped up. My left shoulder was replaced, my right shoulder rebuilt and both of my hips replaced. It took years to be able to walk without devices.

I was very ill, and I didn't know what was coming. It was only going to get worse. I'd be fighting for my life for the next 15 years.

My wife saves my life

After surgery for my first hip replacement, I was wheeled back to my room, hooked up to IVs, cables and wires and left to rest. My wife was at the hospital, but had stepped out while the nurses got me situated.

She came back into the room and my cheeks were sucked in, my chest was full of air and my face was turning black. I had stopped breathing.

My wife hit the emergency button. The staff rushed in, saw what was happening, and told her this was going to get violent and asked her to leave.

When I woke up, there was blood all over the walls and all of my tubes and cables were torn off me. To this day, I don't know all they had to deal with to bring me back. I do know that God, my Father, had used my wife to save me. Praise Him!

This recounting can only cover a small part of the illnesses and suffering unleashed upon me. I've nearly died dozens upon dozens of times over the past two decades.

Kidney failure soon kicked in, then kidney cancer, pulmonary embolisms, Osteonecrosis (dying of the bones) from the meds, pancreatitis, Graves' disease and many other issues. I had a heart attack and three stents were put in my heart. So many surgeries I've lost count. My medical bills would pay a good starting major league pitcher for a couple of years.

Pulmonary embolism

I was with my wife and son for Parker's eleventh birthday at a local amusement park, celebrating. I was in a wheelchair because I struggled walking, especially through the large amusement park on a hot day.

My son and I got on a ride that would spin two side-by-side chairs in the air on chains, a gentle ride I knew I could handle.

The ride took off smoothly and we were laughing, then I suddenly felt a bright, sharp pain in my right lung and I could not breath. It felt like a knife going into my chest. I could barely take in enough air to stay conscious. The pain was unbearable.

The ride stopped and I barely made it back to where my wife was. One look, and she knew I was in trouble.

There was no ambulance or even medics near us in that part of the amusement park so we were on our own. My wife tried to push me in the wheelchair up a steep hill to the parking lot and a Marine thankfully saw her struggling to push me, and jumped in to push me to the parking lot. Medical personnel were summoned, but I was barely hanging on and it took 45 minutes for the medical to reach me.

They couldn't give me pain meds because, due to what they suspected was happening, they'd soon have to use a dye that had stopped my heart in the past.

The pain was so bad I went into shock. I remember

the EMT holding a long needle in his hand and he was on the phone with the hospital. I started losing consciousness and he told me to stay alert.

"Don't let go!" he said, "We have 10 seconds to make it I'm going to have to thrust this needle into your heart."

He started counting down, 10 seconds came and went, as I drifted off.

He thrust that needle so hard through my chest, startling me alert again with adrenaline. That's all I remember from that moment. I was delirious.

They had to pre-med me because of my allergies to the dye. The pain was horrid, and it seemed like it would never end. They ran tests and I was finally diagnosed with a massive pulmonary embolism in my lung. The doctors were surprised I made it through, given where and how it happened. Jesus saved me again!

CHAPTER FOURTEEN

BETWEEN THE REALMS

While I was at home in a hospital bed, and could barely walk, I began reading the bible daily, praying for help. I was so very sick and I knew I was fighting to stay alive. I was lying in bed because I really couldn't walk and would often fall asleep with the bible on my chest.

Once, I was dreaming of two of my relatives talking about a business transaction in real estate and a third person entered the dream. It was a man who had evil written all over him. He frightened me so much I woke from the dream immediately.

I opened my eyes, no longer dreaming, yet this man, this demon, stood over me. Jet black hair, big black eyes and a cool, malevolent delight on his face as he looked at the fear on my face.

It was like he was ready to devour me. He wore a white pinpoint button down dress shirt. This demon was so dark, so evil! His eyes were the size of half dollars but had no pupils. His spiffy dark clothes made his particular brand of evil seem somehow official. I can't explain it fully. It was a waking nightmare. Purely death!

How could a malevolent presence in a dream be standing in my room when I wake up, the dream-realm and reality overlapping?

I was so scared I screamed and my wife came and opened the door and the demon went straight into the floor like some magic trick. I knew he wanted me dead.

Unfortunately, I'd deal with him again.

Another time, praying and reading scripture, I was laying on my couch. I was terribly sick and I fell asleep, again, with the bible on my chest. I dreamt, and the demon appeared.

He grabbed my body, dragging me, spinning through the family room, through the living room and then past the front door to the house in the entryway. I struggled as he rushed me through the dining room and kitchen completing the circle back to the family room.

This demonic journey spun me so violently through these rooms, I was screaming, crying. It couldn't have lasted long, but the minutes seemed to somehow drag throughout it, as if I were somehow stuck in time.

When I woke up, I was on the floor across the room from the couch I'd dozed off in. My body was twisted in a heap, as if I'd been tossed mid-spin. I sat up, looked around the room, confused. I fell back onto my back, grasping and terrified, feeling violated and filthy.

I climbed the stairs, tore off my clothes and got into a hot shower, wanting to cast off this feeling of filthiness. I finished, stepped out and was toweling myself off when I noticed three scratch marks on my chest. I stood there, bewildered. How could a dream demon leave contusions on my body?

The dream realm crossing over into reality, the spiritual realm manifesting on the flesh of my chest!

I need to do something, but what? I thought of scenes in movies like The Exorcist, and had an idea. I walked throughout the house, blessing each room in some approximation of what I'd seen in the movies, trying to stave off any more demonic encounters... but it only would get worse.

I knew God, and worshiped Him, yet, I didn't know enough to fight off these attacks. In the normal course of things, my mind and my fix-it nature would have set me to task to gather info, but I was baffled, frozen in my ignorance.

I do understand that Christ carried me even when I didn't have the tools to know how to do battle within this realm, but, convinced more than ever that the unseen realm exists, I needed to learn if I could. I also needed to depend on Jesus like I never had before.

If I didn't, I would be dead. I know this for a fact.

CHAPTER FIFTEEN

FADING AS THE BATTLE RAGES

Some weeks later, a friend stopped by to show me his motorcycle. He knew I'd always loved bikes and wanted to show off his new acquisition.

With his blessing, I took the motorcycle for a spin. It was tough on me, with all my limb replacements... but I rode around and even managed to have a bit of fun at it.

When I got off the bike, my friend said his goodbyes and pulled out of the drive. As soon as he was out of sight, I started getting really sick, and cripplingly lethargic. I could barely breathe, but I had the presence of mind to get into the house and check my blood pressure, even if I barely had the energy to do so. My blood pressure had fallen to 60/40. I was foggy and weak, and getting weaker by the moment.

My heart rate slowed to 40 beats per minute. My wife piled me and my son into the car and took me to the emergency room, where my vitals had not improved. The doctors put me into the Intensive Care Unit.

I was dying, I could sense it.

I remember looking at my wife with great concern and fear in her eyes. I shook my head. I wasn't going to make it.

I was sadly resigned to the reality of the situation, but our young son, Parker, was in the room, and I didn't want to verbalize the reality of my dire state in front of him. My wife seemed to understand the situation. Her sorrow was palpable, and it sent me into action.

I began praying fervently for help from Jesus. I was so weak I couldn't even cry, but my prayer life had been growing, and I had begun to constantly pray throughout most days.

I knew that only God could keep me alive, the only question would be if that was what He wanted to do. I was totally dependent on Jesus.

I also knew that only He had the authority to take me home to Heaven, and if that was His will, so be it.

I fell into a subdued peace, knowing that one way or the other, my Lord was going to see me through. In my calmed state - what the bible calls a peace that surpasses understanding, I fell asleep.

A few hours later I woke up with the medical staff in the room, but without any sense of urgency or panic. My heart rate and blood pressure had returned to normal and stabilized.

Jesus saved me again.

CHAPTER SIXTEEN

LOSING MY FAMILY

During these years of extreme illness, my interactions with my family soured. I was in pain, worn out, frustrated and angry, and it came out in a horribly sharp tongue with my wife, and even my son. I was verbally mean and abusive.

I hate that it's true, and would give anything to be able to go back and fix it all, but in the maddening impact of my many varied illnesses and their symptoms, I was beyond not nice. I was awful to the love of my life and my son, both of whom I cherish to this day.

My wife had the grace to try to understand what I was going through, and she was long-suffering as my mouth continued to spew out the pain bottled up inside me, but it was more than anyone would want to bear.

I prayed to God to help me do better with my family before I would talk to them... and then I would find myself caustically arguing with my poor son and wife, feeling like no one could relate to my pain and turmoil, believing that their attempts to comfort and advise me were condescending and lacking in empathy.

They weren't, but that's where my head was. I'm not proud of it now and I wasn't then either. I would hurt them, then go back to my room and cry terribly.

I didn't understand what was happening. I love my family with all my heart. I couldn't have a nice conversation, or maintain a proper demeanor at all. My disposition was suspicious, troubled, and buried in physical pain and demonic visions and dreams. Although I didn't want to hurt them, and would never want to, I did hurt them. Over and over.

This went on for years. I could not understand, the demon would show up, not just in my dreams, but in my room, crossing the realms again, and scare me beyond belief.

I would wake up with his face inches from mine, smiling an evil smile. He knew I was spiraling, and my family suffering, and it pleased him. His eyes were the essence of evil, penetrating with a deep darkness like a vast, cold, bottomless lake filled with fathoms of evil, enjoying suffering.

I hated where and how I was. I was terrified and could see all that I'd wanted in life was slipping away from me, but was powerless to stop it.

One day I was ranting and screaming and I picked up and threw a television, breaking it, angry that I was in pain and this evil presence kept showing up to mock me, relishing my hurting.

My family was afraid as I acted out, and I was so mad I insisted my wife and my son drop me off at the interstate. I declared I was leaving. I was so discombobulated and hurt inside, drowning in real pain and self pity.

I wanted to hear my wife tell me she loved me and wanted me to stay... but she didn't. She'd suffered so, and part of her just wanted to be free of the whole thing. I made it back home, but was discouraged, convinced in my self pity that I wasn't wanted.

I don't blame her or hold anything against my dear wife. Every bit of it was me and I was lost. I'm not saying that was fair or right, just reality.

Illnesses, surgeries, medical crises, weariness, fear, and a constant onslaught of demonic attacks all compounded to make me anything but the man I wanted to be during that time.

I knew I was a decent man in my heart but my anger and verbal outbursts were out of control. The devil now seemed to have control of my emotions even when I knew better than to allow it.

He was killing my health, terrifying me with visitations, and had severed the communication between me and the most precious people in my life.

I could not take it anymore, I did not want to live, Of course, having not experienced what I was dealing with, no one in my family could fully understand, and felt isolated, all alone. It was the end.

I was so fed up and out-of-control with anger, tired of the demon plaguing me, that one evening I decided to get smashed on alcohol.

I hadn't drrank in years and my wife was across town at a family gathering. We weren't getting along because of me and I called my wife, arguing with her on the phone, telling her I was going to kill myself.

I drank a lot of vodka that evening and I truly intended to take my life. In my mind, I remember thinking "If I can't have peace with my family, and this demon tortures me endlessly, leaving me with only ugly interactions, pain and fear! I'm just done. Finished. Unworthy and without hope. I might as well die!"

Hammered on the vodka, and close to passing out, I staggered into the kitchen and took a long knife from the knife holder to cut my wrist so I would bleed to death. I know I got the knife, but I don't remember much after that.

I must've passed out at some point. When I woke up, I saw that I hadn't sliced my wrist, I'd cut the top side of my arm, not the underside. I remember thinking "I can't even kill myself correctly," then I blacked out.

Those were the worst days of my life. I was so sick and angry that I was unable to financially support my family. I hated it, and the devil had me convinced I was a loser and that's all I would be now. He'd broken me.

My health continued deteriorating. After all of my verbal abuse, my wife and I separated. She and our son couldn't take it anymore and I do not blame them. No one should go through what I was putting them through.

My wife bought a townhouse and moved out; in my heart I was convinced that it was all over, and I started seeing someone. I convinced myself it was an acceptable choice, believing my marriage was over.

But we weren't yet divorced. I committed adultery, twice, telling myself that I needed companionship and had been abandoned, but those were just excuses, justifications.

It was sin, pure sin, and in my heart of hearts, I knew it.

Deep down, in my conscience, the excuses held no sway. I was horrified that I had committed the sin. I knew it was wrong, and did it just the same. I could have not committed adultery.

On top of the mess I'd made of our marriage, I had become addicted to several of my prescribed medications, and the venture back into alcohol was holding me now, too.

I checked into a rehab to clean up, but my health worsened there. I came out requiring more surgeries and more meds. It would be years before I would stop drinking and could walk without heavy pain meds.

I know what I did now. It was wrong.

It served as the coup de grace for our marriage, and we divorced. It was a tragedy I can't even express properly. My wife is still the love of my life, the one I didn't and don't want to ever be without, but here we are.

We are, as much as she'll allow, friends, and I'm willing to live out my life that way - but knowing it didn't need to have this outcome hurts. I wish our little family could've survived my long season of pain and ugliness.

No one understands what has happened to me other than my best friend, Pastor Hogan. We've known each other for years, but in the aftermath of the marital separation, God led me to join the church Hogan pastors and serve there.

The pastor has been with me when visions have occurred, and God has used him to speak into my life, helping me survive the mess in my wake.

I do not blame my wife for leaving me. I was a mess. I tried to leave me, too, but Jesus would not let me.

I suffer every day with the loss of my marriage. I'm still in love with my wife to this day. When the Lord calls me, I'll leave this world with a broken heart. I believe it will be better, joyous, where He'll take me from here.

After the divorce, the demon's attacks ramped up. He would wake me from my sleep, staring at me, smiling coldly at my dismay and circumstance, then disappear.

Peace escaped me. I was afraid to sleep because I knew the demon would show up, and if he did while I was asleep, he'd likely cross the realms and be in the room when I'd awaken from the dream.

I knew on some level that I couldn't just whither, treading water, resigned to misery and no path forward, so I began to dig into God's word every day, praying for relief.

I was struggling, for sure, but I began to feel safe while in God's word, serving in church activities, and while praying. This realization brought a real change in approach to my days, one which isn't exactly filled with happiness all of the time, but one where I have a sense of wellbeing despite living circumstances that I would have never wanted in life.

Circumstances that are a consequence of my own actions and troubles.

I know God protected me through all of this. As the Lord has drawn me closer, He has reviewed all these events in my life and told me that He continues to renew me, carrying me through all of these attacks and illnesses I've had to deal with.

I would not be alive to this day without the loving and tremendous healing power of Jesus Christ, He continues to save me to this day.

CHAPTER SEVENTEEN

THE CHURCH

I experienced so much sickness, continuing on with more different, dramatic issues. For years, I was hospitalized at least every other month. To this day, I am in the hospital quite often with new and old illnesses.

Many years ago, while I was in the hospital, the man who would become my dear friend showed up to visit me. He'd moved from California and planted an urban church in the Pittsburgh area, and the pastor of the church my wife and I went to had become friends with him.

One time, before they started regular Sunday services, his worship band had come to our church to lead worship, and I played drums with them. I had a blast doing it.

He'd been a professional musician in Southern California, and, with that same type of background, we had much in common and hit it off well.

As I was ill, he would visit me often in the hospital. I

would be there for weeks, sometimes months, and have no visitors except for Pastor Hogan and his assistant Pastor David. He's been by my side through years of helping and praying for me.

I was in need of a church and Pastor Hogan's church was an obvious fit. His church, Faithbridge Community Church, is located in a part of Pittsburgh riddled with crime, violence and death, a place in dire need of the good news of salvation and Jesus's healing power. It is so rough there, the FBI ranked this town, McKees Rocks, among the most violent towns in America.

The school last year had a 9% reading efficiency rating. This means only 1 out of 10 students can read, yet they have a 97% graduation rate - which means they push unprepared people out into the world with a piece of paper that claims they're ready for further education and/or jobs.

Most of the kids don't have two parents raising them, and many are being raised by a grandmother or other family members due to drugs, alcohol, jail or death from overdoses or murder. It is not uncommon for very young kids to carry loaded weapons on the street.

Death and murder are so common here that the people are used to it. They've just adjusted to having people in their lives be forever gone in a hail of gunfire, and they move on as if nothing has happened. It is unimaginably sad!

I had never experienced anything like this place

despite my life of travels. Even more sad is that realization that many other impoverished urban towns suffer the same issues across our nation. Evil runs rampant in this town. It can be dangerous for any and all that live here.

I know of women that have been raped just walking in the streets to go to the laundromat or corner store. Some have even been in their homes and criminals have barged in to rob and rape them.

Very few folks end up prosecuted in this town. The system is broken, the cops too few, the county DA and magistrates too lenient. Folks commit crimes only to be returned to the streets to commit more violence.

In the past two years more than 20 teachers have been hospitalized by student attacks in the joint jr/sr high school here. Our church sits just across the street from the school and we have had gang fights, group attacks and stabbings behind our church.

I recently saw a police officer surrounded by these kids and pushing him around, threatening to kill him as school let out, until other police arrived as backup. It isn't even safe to be a cop in this town!

The kids are troubled, four and five generations removed from the normalcy of two-parent homes, so far in the pit dug for them by other's choices that they can't catch a glimpse of how good a normal, decent life can be.

Most don't respect police, or any authorities, considering them the enemy. Drugs are openly sold on each corner and many parents of these kids are strung out or dealing. Drug addicts wander the streets like zombies, their opioid-damaged voices barely audible, their bodies bent and broken. It's a sad and extremely dangerous place especially at night.

CHAPTER EIGHTEEN

PROVERBS, MY FAILING LITMUS TEST

The first men's bible study I attended at Faithbridge community church was amazing. I'd been struggling with depression from my situation, and physically extremely ill. I had been reading from the book of Proverbs, but not with joy.

I was stuck. I couldn't get out of this book in the bible. I felt like it was trapping me, sitting in judgment of me.

Every time I would read Proverbs it was like a personal, painful litmus test. I'd failed terribly with my family. I was disabled and no longer could work, constantly hospitalized, I felt like a total loser and failure.

I broke down and told the men about my situation reading Proverbs and how it was tearing me up inside. Pastor Hogan asked the men to put their hands on me and prayed for the release from the evil trapping me, and I found myself dumbfounded. It felt like drawing a deep, cool breath of fresh air after struggling to get any oxygen at all for a long while.

After the prayer, I was freed. He addressed the evil, and commanded it away from me in Jesus's name, and I felt like I was finally able to gather some steam, and have some peace again in life.

I now know the demon that caused my depression and spiritual attacks. This demon's name is *"pain"*. I will go further into this later, but it was a real revelation for me.

I soon settled down into the church, becoming a member of the worship team, playing drums or keyboards, fitting in wherever needed.

Faithbridge Community Church is an odd church, filled with people of many ethnic races. A bible-believing church, driven to impact this tough place, living firmly in God's word, for Jesus Christ.

We truly are a family. And, often, a spiritual hospital. Many sick, homeless and addicted or recovering members attend the church, seeking healing from the traps of addiction or from illnesses. This community has a lot of mental health issues - a consequence of the county populating a tiny town on the city line of Pittsburgh with four low-income housing projects for most of a century, where they've shuffled off mentally and intellectually challenged people for decades. Those folks have kids, and, if their issues are genetic, another generation of the issues surfaces. It is so sad.

I understand the term "zombies" now in a sense I was unaware of prior to coming here. After years of drugs and alcohol and abuse many have given up.

Our church steps in to help. We serve God's suffering people, but it's a battle. The same people ripe for help might steal a purse from the pews if the chance arises.

The doors open with opportunities to be a blessing, and with real challenges almost every time. Many tears are shed in this church during service and folks need wise counsel in so many areas. It can be heartbreaking, but it's an essential lifeline back to potential and freedom, if the folks in need are able to hang in there long enough for it to happen.

There are many good people that have lost their way through addiction and ending up with severe mental damage. We serve the Lord with outreaches for the community. This church is helping keep this town alive with hope and love. We are seriously in the middle of a war zone.

One time after worship rehearsal, I walked out of our old church building, a few blocks down the street from where we are now, and I heard gunshots very close by. I told the worship team to stay in and lock down.

I ran to my car. As I was leaving a male youth was standing in front of me with a full face covering and carrying a shiny silver gun. He pointed it at me, but let me drive by.

I don't know why he didn't kill me, except that God was with me.

These types of events occur often here. Children are often armed and often other children become the victims. Elderly folks' houses have been raided and sometimes the old folks end up beaten, raped or murdered.

It is so tough that Pastor Hogan was removed from church one time because a contract was put on his life and the police warned him when they got wind of it. Thankfully, the potential hitman had refused the job, recognizing that it would hurt the town, where he has family members who benefit from what the church does, to act upon it.

We stand for peace and righteousness, led by scripture and the Holy Spirit to serve others and pray continuously. The devil hates us, no doubt. Our safety is in Jesus Christ. He is our Savior and our Protector.

CHAPTER NINETEEN

GOD BEGINS ILLUMINATING

I kept attending Faithbridge Community Church for about a year, but to be transparent, I was having difficulty adjusting to the area and turmoil. Through all my travels I have never seen or experienced all of the unimaginable issues and violence in this town. I was afraid.

People constantly ask for money wherever you turn in this town and the violence is unreal. If you don't give them money, many will get angry. I could not take it anymore. I tend to give even when I can't really spare a dime, and because of that I had been taken advantage of countless times and was tired of it. I felt I should leave the church.

I met with Pastor Hogan before church to discuss my feelings. We talked about our worldview. We're both politically conservative and tend to believe that helping others in the wrong ways tends to do more damage than good. It leaves them dependent and stilted.

In a moment of real enlightenment for me, Pastor Hogan said, "Sometimes our own ideology will keep us from the depths of God - because we cherish our ideology enough to have it disrupt our theology and our methodology."

When he started sharing his thoughts on this, I immediately saw two clear cylinders appear before me, off a bit to my left, floating in the air. They were similar to large test tubes but sealed on both ends, empty and clear.

When Pastor Hogan said the word "ideology," the tubes filled up a quarter way up with a green liquid. He must've seen me looking distracted and said, "stay with me here" and went on explaining how his own politics have to be secondary to his call and God's mission, because it would alienate the majority of the folks here, where God had called him to come and reach the lost. I watched the green in the tubes drain out, disappearing. Again, the tubes were clean.

My mind raced. I'd never seen or experienced visions from God while I was awake. In fact, the only visions and dreams I had experienced weren't of God at all. It had always been the malignant demons trying to kill me.

I was replaying the vision God had just put before me, not sure how to properly process it.

I landed on the thought that God was confirming how my ideology was holding me back in my spiritual life, and I felt the fear and frustration leave me, as did the thought of leaving my church home.

I was flooded then and there with the presence of the Holy Spirit running through me, and my senses were heightened like never before. My awareness of my surroundings was sharper, oddly different, safe, and spiritually full.

The colors around me were magnificent, clear and bright.

I had never felt anywhere near this way before. It was as if the Lord took the blinders off my heart and soul, opening a new world, a glimpse at the other, light-laden side of a spiritual world that I'd never known except for dark demon attacks.

We had to get next door to the Worship Center for service. Pastor Hogan and I walked in the church together. We played the music and led the congregation in worship, then I took my usual spot at the soundboard for the message.

All this time I was in the spirit, something I'd always sort of longed for, but had not really believed in.

In fact, in the past I had stood in front of a men's group in my old church and said I did not believe in new visions or prophecies, that all of the answers that we need are only in the bible. Boy was I wrong!

We took the Lord's Supper together as a congregation, and when my turn arrived, I stood up and got in line. I always waited for last because I was at the soundboard

in the back of the sanctuary. As I shuffled forward with
the line, I then heard the voice of Jesus. A voice I know
so dearly now. He speaks to me with such grace and
gentleness, with the divine wisdom and perspective of
the ages. It's never been threatening, but since I first
heard it, it's always been direct and uncontestable.

Jesus said, "Look at my people."

Immediately raising my eyes to the folks walking
back from receiving the elements - the unleavened
bread and wine - Jesus showed me souls. The souls of
the folks I worship with and among, including Pastor
Hogan, folks I knew well and others I barely knew
at all.

I could see parts of the framework of folks' skeleton,
the girdering that allows us to be upright in stature even
when we might be falling apart at the seams inside. The
soft tissue was blacked or grayed out.

It seemed almost as if everyone were wearing some
kind of black cut off top, small and thin enough to
glimpse the structural bones. I could see where the
neck bones met the spine. Below that, in the center of
the chest, everyone had a bright oblong yellow light. I
recognized the shape.

It was the same shape as the tubes I'd see fill and
drain as they hovered in the air in the pastor's office.

The soul!

For His own reasons, God was allowing me to see
something rare and usually off-limits to humans, the

very core of the human being. Inside the souls of my fellow worshipers were tears. They filled the bottom of the tubular shape. Hundreds of tears.

The Holy Spirit let my spirit know these tears are the scars and wounds of the trials and suffering one goes through in life.

All the pain and suffering, gathered down in their souls as tears. The pooled tears had a bluish hue, but above those I could see one large teardrop, round and blue as well, shining with the bright light of the soul. The light was brilliant, nearly blinding, but the tears were visible.

It would be several days before I came to understand what this big round tear means.

The next week I stood outside the church talking to others. A church member raised his hands as he emphasized a point, and I was shown the soul again, his soul.

Jesus spoke, telling me about the big teardrop.

"This is my love for you. Agapé love." I'd heard the word before, probably even heard it defined, but now my eyes welled up and my chest swelled as I felt God's perfect love for us. God's agapé love is perfect, described in the bible. I was overwhelmed at what God was showing me.

> Love suffers long *and* is kind; love does
> not envy; love does not parade itself, is not

> puffed up; **5** does not behave rudely, does not seek its own, is not provoked, thinks no evil; **6** does not rejoice in iniquity, but rejoices in the truth; **7** bears all things, believes all things, hopes all things, endures all things. **8** Love never fails. ~1 **Corinthians 13:4-8**

I broke down in the church building by myself, crying and praising Jesus, thanking Him for these interactions and visions as the privilege and wonder of what He was allowing to happen in my life rolled over me in waves of elation.

I remember doubting visions, even thinking people who claimed to experience them were lying or evil. Now God was expanding my understanding, spiritually, mentally and emotionally.

I went to God's word.

> 'And it shall come to pass in the last days, says God, That I will pour out of My Spirit on all flesh; Your sons and your daughters shall prophesy, Your young men shall see visions, Your old men shall dream dreams. ~**Acts 2:17**

My soul changed in these interactions. I can't fully explain the depths of the change, because I believe on some level the spirit grasps it in ways the brain and our normal communication tools fall short of, but I knew Jesus wanted me to remain with the church. My heart and soul opened to the community in new ways of empathy and grace that had been foreign to me before. I feel the pain of the members of this community now.

I love them. I am with them. I am changed.

As time went on Pastor Hogan and I drew closer, and God used it to open new doors of life for me, doors I never anticipated with my health challenges and how my anger and outbursts had burned my most important relationships with my wife and son.

This was the beginning of a new world, and new life for me. A spiritual life in Christ, a life I never believed in for real, nor knew. When God redeems us, we are truly redeemed and the second chances are more tangible than I ever understood.

I was living alone and my heart was torn up. I was, and am still, extremely sad over the loss of my family. Weary from constantly fighting for my life in and out of the hospital, I felt misunderstood.

Dreams and visions began to occur more often, becoming nearly constant.

Many of them came from God's beautiful revelation of things I needed to gain and experience for all He desired for me to do in His name, but the demonic intrusions would still harass me, torturing me and pounding me with illness and depression despite God's equipping me better.

This Is Your Life

The informing, emboldening visions from God and the ugly spiritual intrusions from the demonic realm seemed an ironic and confusing, completely opposite juxta positioning of light and darkness, good and evil.

When God would give me visions, even when they were challenging, I trusted they were for my good, and for the good of others and came away with an ever deepening trust of Him and gratitude for the enlightenment. When the devil invaded my dreams or manifested in my room, it was always terrifying and angering to me. The tension between these two things was real and straining to dwell upon in my mind.

Why did I suffer demonic intrusions when God made it so clear that I belong to Him, He is using me for His glory, and He loves me?

God gave me the answer one day.

It was life and perspective changing, giving me an entirely different view of my entire life history, God's love for me, and awakened - at God's miraculous hand - memories and details long lost decades ago.

The DC bureaucrat I mentioned at the start of this

book appeared on a news report, and, as usual, I had a visceral reaction to him. It's unlike my reaction to anyone else, palpably distasteful and vile. I heard God say, "It's him," not understanding, yet, what He meant. Then God grabbed ahold of my spirit and mind and took me on a mental journey back through time. It reminded me of the premise of the old This Is Your Life television program from my younger years.

God showed me demonic attacks throughout my life, beginning all the way back when I was a toddler, that had been directed by the devil.

He showed me scenes from memories long ago washed from my head, details I couldn't possibly remember. The bright colors of the sun shining down through the pool water as I drifted toward the bottom as a toddler; the actual action of my small hand properly locking the station wagon car door on the day I was thrown from the car; the sound of the crying children in the cancer ward - and much, much more.

Some things that had been traumatic and difficult during my life weren't shown to me. Emergency surgery to remove my appendix, various typical childhood schoolyard clashes, challenging days in the automotive industry where I was tasked with letting go of entire departments due to lax bosses who'd allowed standards to fall to liability level, etc. All of these things (and many more) were hard, but none revisited at God's behest on this day.

No, only the things engineered by the devil and his minions were brought back that day, as God showed me how intensely the devil has desired to upend my life since birth.

No, I hadn't just had a revved up nighttime imagination that caused horrid dreams, and, yes, as I ran up the hill to my house harassed by demons I was actually being harassed by demons.

Illnesses that derailed my livelihood, planes tumbling from the sky, and the sum total of illness and isolation being egged on by the actual presence of a demon in my house when I woke from being bothered in my dreams leading to me lashing out at those I love the most. All of it deviously planned and purposed to harm or even kill me, to make me ineffective in what God desires for my life.

"The devil has wanted you dead from birth," God said, bringing to my mind Jesus telling Peter of how the devil had wanted to sift him away from Christ like a miller separating chaff out of wheat. "I have renewed you everytime."

I knew, with not one scintilla of doubt, the truth of what God had said. I sat there, amazed at the intense, high definition detail God had brought out of old, faded, even lost, memories, startled that so much had not been just the way of the world and the luck of the draw... but positive it was exactly as God had just shown me.

I shuddered thinking about being under attack as a baby, then throughout my life. Then I shook it off. God had seen me through! I may be quite worse for wear, but no one gets through this life unscathed. I can relish the truth that God has fought battles on my behalf, kept me under his care and carried me through so much.

Hard to believe

My own family struggles to believe me. Some, absent any relationship or concern for the things of God, just count me as nutty.

Feeling bad one day about how few people would bother visiting me in the hospital, and how ostracized I sometimes felt, I was dwelling on the idea that people I love doubt me and/or think the bolts in my brain have come undone. In my sadness at this, Jesus intervened.

"My own people didn't believe Me," He said, "Your family doesn't believe you, but people will."

That is why I am writing this book. I knew and trusted that despite life's challenges, Jesus is with me. Because of him, I could survive what was coming.

CHAPTER TWENTY

KIDNEY CANCER ATTACKS

Always fighting illness and realizing I wasn't in good enough health to drive, I decided to take the train to see my daughter, my son in-law and my grandsons in New Jersey.

I figured it would be fun to take a train, and I had been so sick that it was likely the best way to travel.

My father, a writer and newsman, had written an article many years before about the great train wreck at Horseshoe Curve near Altoona PA, and as the train cut across the Pennsylvania countryside, we passed through the curve.

It was a delightful reminder of my father, just knowing he had been here to gather material for his story. I miss my folks, gone now. I often miss my parents and my brothers and sisters, too. All of us many years into our own lives. I love them, even if they don't understand me much.

I had a tremendous week with my daughter, my

son in-law and my two grandsons, touring their area and having a blast with the boys. After a week, I took the train back to Pittsburgh. When we pulled into the station, I tried to stand up, but my legs wouldn't move. Pain shot down to my feet as I tried to get my legs in gear.

A fellow passenger helped me get up and out of the car, and I made it to my vehicle, but it was extremely difficult getting in my car.

I thought "once I am in the car, I won't be able to get out," and it proved true. I drove to the emergency room. They had to lift me out of my car. I couldn't walk.

The staff pumped me full of pain killers so I could move and respond. I was guessing my back was out. Maybe, given the pain, even totally shot.

The hospital ran blood tests, cat scans and an MRI. We all believed it was my back. The tests came back and it wasn't my back.

I had kidney cancer, a large tumor on my right kidney.

My kidneys have been in rough shape for years. Doctors say I am usually in kidney failure, I had already been treated with chemo once for kidney issues and now this happened.

They couldn't remove my kidney because of my kidney disease - the other one couldn't handle the load. The kidney with cancer was still functioning at some level, but I needed both kidneys.

I was in trouble.

Since they could not remove my kidney, they did a procedure called an oblation on my right kidney. Basically, they burned the tumor off of the kidney. Despite the procedure being deemed successful my overall health was getting worse and worse.

I'd already had a major pulmonary embolism, a heart attack and three stents put in my heart. Osteonecrosis had killed much of the bone in my jaw. My shoulders and hips were either removed and replaced or reconstructed.

My bones, due to the medication I'd been prescribed, were still dying and kidney failure was on the edge of taking me down.

All of my doctors agree that I needed to get all of my care through one location so the doctors could better coordinate. They turned me over to UPMC in the city of Pittsburgh.

My doctors are some of the best doctors in the world, which was good. I needed their expertise to survive.

I was literally dying, and the doctors told me they'd never seen anyone survive as long as I had with the damage level I'd suffered from that particular medication and illnesses at such a rapid rate. At my old doctor's office, not related to UPMC, a nurse told me that some of the staff had had a poll on my life. How long I would live. Like a football poll.

I can't believe they did that, I thought they were my friends. But, I suppose dealing with crisis and death must callous a person's emotions. Hearing it was tough on me, though. It upset me so much I had to go home and pray and cry, asking Jesus to save my soul and my life. Praise the Lord I am at UPMC. God has used these doctors to save my life again and again.

I was so sad all the time in my heart but I kept it to myself except for talking with Pastor Hogan and my friend, guitar player Matt Barranti.

I hadn't had three months in 12 years free of hospitalization. I had spent well over a year of my life in the hospital by this time. More time there awaited.

CHAPTER TWENTY- ONE

THE GOOD NEWS PLACE

As time went on, a friend of mine who is an incredible evangelist, Sam Miller, a commercial plumber by trade, had a dream.

Sam wasn't from this town either, but had been involved in a couple of organizations Faithbridge was associated with - MadDaDDs, a street patrol anti-violence group and Acts Men, a gathering of men chasing after a better understanding of God's word together.

In his dream. Jesus Christ was facing Sam and asked, "Do you love me?"

Sam said yes, yet Jesus asked again, then several more times before Jesus told him, "Feed my people".

So, Sam rented a storefront in town and gathered a team together to feed the needy, teach the bible, and provide a safe place for folks to hang out.

Every Monday, Wednesday and Friday we provide lunches for the needy and homeless.

This ministry is called The Good News Place. We hold men's and women's recovery meetings and bible studies there. This has been going on for five years and, after the church was blessed to purchase a much bigger facility, it is now located in the Worship Center's downstairs Fellowship Hall.

The program has been a real blessing to this town. It isn't easy. While it was at the storefront, there were several times we had to lock down because of nearby gunfire.

One evening down there, the pizza shop next door called us and told us that a man in his shop was claiming, right then, that he was going to head next door and kill us all.

Grateful for the head's up, we locked the doors, paused the bible study and hid in the back room. The Good News Place store front was all window, and we could see him attempting to get in without success.

The police picked him up two blocks away and he was carrying a gun and had a warrant out for his arrest, from across the state in Philadelphia for murder. Jesus, using our Turkish Muslim neighbors at the pizza place, had protected us from a massacre. Praise God!

Many people would not have eaten much without the Good News Place. Often the three days of lunches were the only food many folks in this broken place would eat in a given week. I'd never really seen stuff like that, and it breaks my heart. I know the Lord protects us in this town, which is very good. We must deal with the risks, but can't stop serving. During the Summer, we have children coming in for lunch, saying they don't get to eat since school is out for the Summer Break. Our school district is neither good at education nor safe for the kids, but, due to poverty, it serves essential free meals to students throughout the school year.

Many kids have no home support at all. Dad is M.I.A. and mom is overwhelmed, or high, or often out living her life, leaving the kids to fend for themselves. This, in part, is how gangs form. The longing for support and camaraderie drives young folks to the gangs, and the gang becomes a sort-of surrogate family for them.

Despite my own sufferings, I've learned to often focus outward, as an intercessor for others. This town convicts me. I spend a lot of time in prayer throughout every day, praying for others who suffer and all those in need.

CHAPTER TWENTY-TWO

JESUS SAVES MY SOUL

One evening we were having a bible study at the old Good News location and I was troubled. I had fallen asleep the night before and felt something very evil and dark in my sleep. I woke up and the same old demon was inches away from my face, sporting the grin of sin and death I'd see so often before. I was petrified.

I expressed some emotions, shame and a sense of failure and guilt before the small group of men gathered for the study, and several people chimed in with different thoughts on my situation and how to handle it. Pastor Hogan, however, had the key to my situation.

He said to me, "You've never forgiven yourself for things Jesus has forgiven you of. He's forgotten it 'As far as the East is from the West' but you still cling to it". That hit me right at the core, and I had an angry, guttural response.

I stood up in tears and declared, "I can't forgive

myself!", and stormed out of the building. While I was driving home, I was weeping continuously. I could barely see to drive through the tears.

I had never felt the way I was feeling at that moment and felt like a total loser. A worthless sinner who'd destroyed his family. A man with no more purpose in life, just hanging on to survive.

My sin would constantly run through my mind. I was a loser, nowhere to go, no apparent route up and out of my guilt and misery. That same old demon was constantly coming at me and I felt I had no chance in life to pull myself out of my struggles.

I tried to go back to work, but physically couldn't do it. I would end up back in the hospital. None of this made any sense to me. I went from an executive lifestyle in business with a beautiful family, a beautiful home and found myself with nothing. I was totally broken.

When I got home to my little apartment I sat and I could not stop crying. I remember asking Jesus, "Is this all my life will be? I have no reason to live now, Jesus! Please take me home if this is all there is for me. I am worthless!"

All of my sins and my losses would not leave my mind. I was crying so hard I could not put my emotions into words, was groaning and wailing like a baby, nonstop. I have believed since I was a child that abortion, the killing of a viable, developing human is a horrific affront to God, in whose image we are all created, yet, when I was young and feeling trapped and pressured by circumstance, I was involved in an abortion. The weight of that has always been a heavy one for me, and now as I sat crying out of control, it was heavier than ever. I didn't stand a chance.

I had never cried like this before, so many things to say, yet I found myself unable to put them into words. I curled up on my couch, weeping and groaning like a baby. The pressure in my torso was so intense I was concerned I would have another heart attack unless I got the weeping and groaning under some kind of control. I started begging Jesus to save me, in my mind, as my mouth still seemed unable to form words.

"Please, save my soul and life! Give me a purpose for you, please, I beg of You!"

The next thing I knew I was on the floor. on my hands and knees. I was in the spirit. Right under my chest on the floor was a picture frame. The picture frame was old and worn.

The frame looked like it was made of maple, light brown. It was a perfect square. Inside the frame was black swirling liquid with white stripes. The liquid was spinning counterclockwise, extremely fast. It was draining in the center. Spinning as if you pulled the drain on a sink. I don't know how long I was there, but it seemed like a long time, staring at the picture frame and the swirling

Inside of me, my spirit shouted, "They are all gone!" and I understood.

Jesus Christ was cleansing me, draining my sins. I lifted my head, looking forward and saw the feet of Jesus! I looked up. Jesus was standing in front of me with His arms opened to me, His hands turned up.

He wore a white robe. draping down to the floor. The robe hung open and his clothing underneath were white as well. He had beautiful long brown locks of hair with beautiful curls at their ends, big ones, 3 inches around and His magnificence glowed, shining His glorious light down on me. My spirit leaped inside of me!

The robe had long pleats and the sleeves draped open nearly a foot at His hands. His eyes shone bright blue, his beard short. He was perfect and beautiful. Just looking at Him I could feel total kindness and forgiveness and love emanating from Him.

I sensed somehow that He could feel the sadness and suffering I was going through as He held his arms out to me. I knew He felt my pain. Jesus was there to rescue me, my life, and my soul for eternity.

He loved me.

Sensing that at a time in my life when I thought the experience of love, being in love, being loved and living in love was gone forever, was humbling and amazing. I had been suffering for a long time, years... but now my Savior is here!

I barely had any control of myself. When I saw Jesus, I literally jumped up from being down on all four and leaped onto the couch, burying my face in the cushion, crying, overwhelmed in His presence, ashamed of my sin.

"Lord, I couldn't give you my sins because they are ugly and You are perfect. You are clean and holy... and I am filthy. I am not worthy! Yet you save me!

I immediately went into worshiping and praising Jesus, thanking Him for His forgiveness, for taking my sin away, and thanking Him for saving me.

Suddenly, as I lay there on the couch, there was a perfectly shaped water vase floating in the air to my right. Jesus stood in front of me. I pushed myself up to a seated position, in awe.

The vase was solid gold, about a gallon in size, with a thick rim at the top. From its side projected a beautifully curved gold handle.

The gold shone brightly with brilliant color. I was mesmerized, and as I watched the vase tilted, spilling burning hot liquid gold into a large golden bar-like ingot, glowing red from the heat until it quickly cooled.

The ingot was about 8 inches long and even though it was freshly poured, it seemed I could see years of use weathering its sides with shiny scars and scratches, showing it had been through some things, serving some divine purpose. At one end of the rectangle the corners were rounded, burnt off from wear.

The vase hovered a foot above the ingot as fresh, glowing liquid gold continued to pour into it. Although there was no mold, the shape was somehow maintained, only becoming larger as it took on more of the precious metal.

I sat amazed, watching. From my mouth I heard me say "Purify gold," and was mortified that I had interjected in this divine moment.

I cried out, "I am sorry, I don't mean me," stammering for words.

Suddenly a bible flew up into my face.

The bible stopped six inches from my face. I could read Holy Bible on the dark, worn cover of the book. I peered past the bible and could see the top of a man's head, from the forehead up.

The forehead had long lateral wrinkles. This man was ancient. His hair was thin, clearly showing his scalp. His hair draped to his left, and he bellowed "Yes!" to me in a loud, deep gravelly voice, shaking my body with a thunderous concussion, and I nodded in agreement - even though I wasn't sure what I was agreeing to, just that it was correct whatever it was.

Jesus Himself still stood in front of me, only a couple of arm's lengths from me. Thinking that I had His divine audience and something on my heart, I asked Jesus to heal my dear friend.

The room shifted and next to Jesus, now quite a bit further from me in an adjacent room with windowed walls, appeared a body on a stretcher. I was moved suddenly next to Jesus again, inside the clinically white room. Jesus's robe, blown by winds I couldn't feel, swirled around Him like a cloud.

Jesus was facing me and He rolled His hands along the body. Groans escaped His throat as He concentrated on the prone form upon the stretcher. Rolling His hands closed, then opening them again as He worked, He moved up and down the body.

Sensing this work both holy and important, I fell into deep prayer and praised Jesus as He showed me His healing hands at work. I was at peace, yet tingled from head to toe as He did his thing.

This experience changed my life, my soul, my heart and my mind. Raised Catholic, my religious upbringing had been ritualistic and intellectual. I was skeptical of folks who claimed real interactions with God, dubious of folks operating "in the spirit," and suspicious of spiritual claims outside of what I'd personally experienced... and here God was showing me that He didn't fit in the box I'd tried to keep Him in. My mind and spirit were expanding in ways I would never have believed before.

Now I live for Jesus. He is my purpose, my life, my Redeemer and loving Savior who has rescued me.

This experience lasted nearly 6 hours. That was the first night I had slept a real sleep in peace for a long time. No restlessness, no discomfort, no demons or evil dreams.

Saved in actuality, not just some theological thought, rescued from more than just Hades, set on course from divine opportunities and eternal impact, my capacity to worship God launched to a new, unexplored level. I felt freedom in His presence and His presence in the freedom of a walk anew. Praise Jesus! My life is brand new. I am alive for Christ now!

After this experience, my spirit became extremely alert to my surroundings, to all that goes on around me. The world seems a lot brighter to me, cleared now, even to this day.

A spiritual awareness has manifested that God utilizes constantly within me. I sense evil, identifying demonic activities and can sense vulnerability and even oppression and possession in a person's spirit. Jesus has opened up to me a completely different world. The spiritual world written of and talked about in tomes and tales down through the ages - one that I had no grasp of before, but now do. Praise Jesus!

My prayer:

My Heavenly Jesus Christ, I thank You for saving me, my soul, and my body.

Lord, I pray that if anyone is withholding sin, anger, fear or anything else that keeps them from the truth and You, that You touch them as You have touched me. Please let those who suffer as I did know that You are there for them. I pray they call on You, Jesus, never to be alone again. Abiding in Christ I pray this in Your holy name.

Amen

I have always had a consistent daily prayer life. For years it was perfunctory and shallow, but it has changed, becoming deeper and even more rich in the days since I became sick, but my prayer life today is completely different after Jesus touched me.

I treat each and all day as if He, Jesus, is either sitting or walking with me wherever I am. The apostle Paul admonishes the believer to "pray without ceasing," something I honestly thought would never be within my reach, but now I understand. Because He is at my side and He is paying attention. He loves us and longs for our interaction. I pray speaking to Him continuously all day and night, all of the time. What I had before was faith, but faith has now become fact to me. I know Jesus Christ.

CHAPTER TWENTY-THREE

THE DEVIL BRINGS CANCER BACK

One evening I was home after spending the day at church and I was not feeling well. Over the course of minutes I became sicker and sicker. I had my cell phone near my head, but my body was suffering a complete collapse and I didn't have the energy to call for an ambulance.

I was dying.

I laid there going in and out of consciousness, struggling to breathe, my body sore from head to toe.

The phone rang, startling me. I opened my eyes, reached for the phone - right next to me, but seemingly miles away. I finally reached it and I pressed the answer button. It was Pastor Hogan, who lives 25 minutes away. I barely had enough energy to convey, at a whisper, how sick I was, and he immediately came to get me.

When Pastor Hogan arrived, he helped me into the church van. I couldn't sit, so he laid me across the bench seat behind him, and rushed me to the hospital. Unfortunately, because of my medical history, I can really only be treated at Presbyterian Hospital in the Oakland section of Pittsburgh, which is forty minutes from my place, because my whole medical team is based there. The pastor got me there in 25 minutes, pushing the 30 year-old van to its limit.

We arrived at the emergency room. I could not sit up, so I laid on the emergency room floor's tile. I started coughing up blood as I was on the floor. The triage folks didn't have available beds, but they pressed to have a spot cleared and finally got me to a bed. MRI's, x-rays, and cat scans were run on me, as well as multiple tubes drawn for bloodwork. I was admitted.

In a room upstairs, the doctors came to see me with the test results

Kidney cancer. A large tumor had formed and was impacting blood flow and my body's ability to cleanse toxins from my system. The kidney cancer was back.

Even as they shared the diagnosis, I knew Jesus would heal me.

That was a comforting assurance in my spirit, but I was suffering tremendously and the physical pain was terrible. I was injected full of pain and nausea medications, which helped me settle down so I could relax and get my blood pressure under control.

When I was first diagnosed with kidney cancer they sent me to an oncologist named Doctor Gideon. In the bible, Gideon is a man who God sees great potential in despite his own doubts, and becomes a great champion of Israel. Doctor Gideon, serving in Pittsburgh, is from Jerusalem, the holy city in Israel, where Jesus changed the world.

We consulted at that time, but due to his schedule he was unable to do my oblation and had another doctor perform the operation.

This time, as soon as I saw Dr. Gideon, I knew it was confirmation that God was healing me. I was stable now, having my physical turmoil brought into some semblance of outwardly normal status by medicinal intervention, and he decided to run another scan, but allow me to go away for a few days with my sisters at the beach.

We arrived in the Outer Banks on Saturday. I wasn't fully up to snuff, but I trucked along with them, grateful to spend time with family.

I fell asleep Saturday night and dreamt of two giant hands cupped together. Within these two hands was my body. I heard the voice of God, a voice I've learned to know well.

"I am keeping you alive for Me," God said. Wow!

I told my sisters of the dream and early on Monday morning Dr. Gideon called. He said there is nothing to worry about, the scan he had taken before I left showed no sign of the tumor. It was all gone!

I praise you God my Father for saving me again and

again! I knew He was going to heal me and now that was clearly confirmed, not just for me, but for all of my friends who I'd assured of God's intent to heal me, and for the good doctor, Dr. Gideon and his staff, who were amazed.

My New Life

Since the first time I saw Jesus, He has so far shown Himself to me four more times. On top of those interactions, God has told and shown me warnings for His people. I share what He shows me, both for those who know Him, and for those in danger of Hell because they don't.

This is where culture and society will split, and I expect criticism from many. Many folks don't want to think about such, and believe that Christians are condemning, ugly people for daring to share God's truth with them. We're not. We love others, even those who can't stand us, and want folks to know the truth so they can be right with God and find salvation.

I don't care if these truths upset others, if I'm being honest with myself. Once you've interacted with the Creator for real, the slings and arrows, and, in some ways, the feelings of folks who will be angered pale in comparison to the great gift we've been given to offer them.

I care about those who are not saved and what is ahead for them unless they accept Jesus, repent and change their ways. God's ways work. All other ways, whether folks want to hear it or not, don't. They may get a person through life believing that they've carved their own path and made their own rebellious way to the finish line... but it can't get them across the finish line. Only Jesus and His truths can get us out of this life an into the glorious home God hopes we'll all come to to embrace our divine citizenship.

> Jesus said to him, "I am the way, the truth, and the life. No one comes to the Father except through Me. ~**John 14:6**

> This is a command from God to me to write what you are reading.

> These are visions and words from Jesus Christ my Savior and God my Father.

CHAPTER TWENTY-FOUR

THE DEMON NAMED "PAIN"

A few days after meeting with Pastor Hogan and explaining what God has shown me, we stopped at his house. We walked in the front door and I stopped in their family room while Hogan went into the kitchen.

Standing in the family room I fell into the spirit. To my left I saw four perfectly square lots of land.

The background of each of the lots was white. All four connected to make a big square. Each individual square was fenced in on all four sides with wooden posts connected with barbed wire. As I observed this I could hear tremendous screaming and evil cackling.

Each lot held multiple mounds of dirt, and behind each mound was a figure of someone screaming. There were many, many of these figures in each lot, screaming.

I heard myself say, out loud, "Fields of pain" for it was obvious they were all in horrible pain. My vision came up close as if with the zoom function on a camera, and I could see these figures better. They were scary!

The figures' heads were giant, with a few thick, long black hairs coming out of the the top of their heads, trailing down to their waists. The anger in their eyes was palpable, their eyes solid black like death. Their gaping mouths were open impossibly wide, stretching down to their abdomens and they were excruciatingly ugly! Their four-fingered hands swooped and waved in my direction from the ends of their grotesque arms as they screamed at me.

After I said "fields of pain" I heard Jesus's voice correcting me.

He said, "No, *pain's* field."

I looked straight ahead and there He was, standing in front of me. Jesus Christ. Standing next to Jesus was a dark green blob-like creature with one huge eye and one huge horn. This was the demon Jesus called pain. The fields were filled with lesser demons the nearly formless green *"pain"* unleashes on earth.

Horns represents power and strength in the bible. My spirit let me know that this particular demon, *pain*, sends out his evil servants to engender depression, anger, divorce, mental illnesses and other non-physical sufferings. The emotional and spiritual pain that troubles humans in ways other creatures couldn't understand. We're created "Imago Dei," in God's image, with capacites beyond even the angels... but even as this is a privileged, blessed attribute, it also makes us susceptible to things no other species must suffer. Having experienced these demons and the evil work they do in the past, God's revelation gave me a rich, if hard to embrace, understanding of so many folks' plights.

I wondered why exactly Jesus had shown me this until I suffered kidney failure some time later. I was seriously depressed and preparing for three 10-hour infusions of chemo, not wanting to go through it at all because of a dye allergy that could make it dangerous and painful.

I was praying to God and Jesus showed me the vision of the demon *pain* again.

I got it.

Immediately I declared, crying out in the name, and blood, and resurrection of Jesus Christ the demon *pain* disallowed from my presence and bound, removed from me and forbidden to trouble again.

Tears made my vision blurry, but I could see a transparent black film slide up over my body, then past my eyes, then over and off of my head. Immediately I knew I was free.

This is what I have learned. Demons hate us knowing their name. That is why Jesus showed me this, to call *pain* off of me. If you are suffering from depression, accept Jesus as your Savior and command *"pain"* bound by the blood of Christ! You must use the demon's name, it is *pain*. This was the second time Jesus appeared to me.

CHAPTER TWENTY-FIVE

BILLY GRAHAM MINISTRIES AND COVID VISION

I am usually at church seven days a week, either serving or writing and recording original Christian music, but one day I stayed home because of my health.

It was a dreary day and a typical upper Ohio River Valley cold rainy winter day, snowing and cloudy, a Pittsburgh day. At noon I turned on the tv to watch the news on the Christian Broadcasting Network (CBN).

A rumor had been circulating for weeks that some sort of pandemic was hitting China. The date was February 1st, 2020.

The headline for the day was:

Franklin Graham Ministries tour of Europe canceled due to LGBT outrage

I was stunned. It made me nauseous to think that a good-hearted, gospel sharing ministry could be attacked so, and derailed by the very people whose lives could be forever changed and saved by hearing and embracing the message of good news it was meant to bring.

The next thing I knew I was in a deep vision, far from my place.

I was at the double-door entrance of a parts department in a car dealership I had consulted for over the years in Chicago.

On my left, was a wall, painted light yellow. The floors were covered in gray paint. The wall held dark green steel pallet racks, corrugated steel, three rows tall. The racks held perfectly undamaged boxes with lids on them. On the top shelf of the rack, in the very far corner was the only empty spot containing no box.

In the center of the floor sat one box. This box, closed with its lid, said "Billy Graham."

An employee entered the room from the right side, wearing the dealership's usual blue shirt and khakis. He walked in front of me and picked up the Billy Graham box. He carried it to the empty space and put the box there, then startled me by yelling, at the top of his lungs, "It is done!"

Suddenly I heard God say "Pray for the safety of your family."

Fear seized me, concerned for my family. What does this mean? My thoughts were jumbled as I tried to understand.

It was the last box, what does that mean? Is my family in danger? What do they have to do with the late Billy Graham or his son Franklin and his canceled tour of Europe? It was confusing and I was very concerned.

I stopped trying to figure it out, and just decided to obey.

I started praying for all of my brothers and sisters, all of their spouses, children, their children's spouses and their grandkids. I prayed for my dear daughter Lauren, her husband, and my grandsons. I prayed for my dear son Parker, and my ex-wives and their families.

My ex-wife, Parker's mother, soon became extremely ill with Covid-type symptoms. She called the hospital, concerned that it could be the China virus we'd all heard about by now. The hospital was less than concerned. They said that since she hadn't been out of the country recently, it would be impossible to have the new virus, and brushed off her concerns, cutting the call short.

I know she had the virus; she almost didn't make it.

She was bedridden for half a month, and I was sure that this is why God had commanded me to pray for my family. The pandemic is long in our rearview, but I continue to pray for the safety of my family to this day.

CHAPTER TWENTY-SIX

KIDNEY FAILURE, COVID

Six months later I became very sick again.

Kidney failure.

My body was swelling, my thyroid was going haywire. My blood count was bad and I was dumping all of the protein out of my body. No matter what I would ingest, it came out in my urine, leaving bubbles in the toilet like a thick head of beer.

I need to emphasize that I am sick everyday - it's part of my lot in life with the damage to my body - so when I say I got sick again, it's serious. I most likely am fighting for my life. I was so sick that the doctors summoned a world-renowned kidney disease expert to arrive from New York.

When we met, she read my charts and stated she hasn't had a patient this bad off with this disease who has survived beyond 30 days. Most of them, she said, last less than a week, usually 3 days.

She was amazed I was alive through all of the

medical problems I've battled. I have had this disease for 15 years now.

The treatment was once again ten hour infusions of chemotherapy. I went through these treatments while on transplant medications to stop my body's defenses from countering the chemo. I had no immune system at all.

While receiving my third ten-hour dosage I got covid!

I'd sort of figured it was likely to happen because I had no way to fight off anything. They stopped the immunosuppressors, and it was very rough on me, but I got much better rather quickly, other than the usual stuff I have to deal with.

I didn't take any of the Covid vaccines because I trust God and I tend to be allergic to vaccines of all stripes. Flu and pneumonia shots have hospitalized me so there was no way I was signing up for that.

My kidneys, miraculously, began working again. It was a long hard road but once again Jesus saved me. I had told members of the church Jesus would save me because He already has time and again. I actually knew it in my heart from the beginning. I was never in fear of dying because I believed and knew Jesus would heal me. If I did die, well, that would be a win, too, anyway. I'd be with Jesus in heaven.

Evil city, Jesus on the clouds

One day as covid was cranking up and everything was closed, Pastor Hogan and I went up to Mount Washington, overlooking the city of Pittsburgh from across the river. The view is amazing, rated one of the best city views in America.

We went up there to pray for our city. At our church, the people did not want the church shut down. When the governor shut the state down on March 23rd, it was two days before Palm Sunday. We met that day to prayer walk the community. The next Sunday, we weren't about to not celebrate the resurrection of Christ, so we gathered in the Worship Center, read the resurrection accounts from scripture, and took the Lord's Supper. The following Sunday we began meeting again for typical Sunday worship services, and never stopped. We held church every Sunday without exception. Our people understood that faith means trusting Jesus even when the whole world is struggling with fear. They demanded we meet, and we did. God is our protector and we can't close His church while claiming to trust Him.

Mount Washington sits hundreds of feet above the three rivers of Pittsburgh, facing the city. We prayed, then as we finished I thought about all that I've seen and experienced in this town, and I said to myself, "what an evil city, it has deep evil roots.".

Some cults have started here that have led folks away from Christ for over a century.

I was thinking about that as I looked out at the city and suddenly, I saw big black roots shoot up between the buildings and skyscrapers all across the downtown area. The roots raised 100 feet above the skyscrapers. Their ends were hacked level, as if someone had been trying to keep them at bay down at ground level.

The many roots entangled among the buildings were very old and huge. One was as wide and large as the UPMC skyscraper, the largest building in Pittsburgh. It was black and aged and poked out some over all of the other roots, its own edges hacked raw and ragged, too. Then the roots slammed, back down to the city floor and disappeared.

CHAPTER TWENTY-SEVEN

THE DYING STRANGER

After I saw this vision, I went to the Good News Place to help serve lunches and pray for those in need. It was a beautiful summer day and we were busy serving and praying when a man approached us who was extremely confused and drugged up.

I talked to him about his needs and, after several minutes of talking, he stated that he forgot to mention it, but he thinks his friend just died across the street in an empty lot. Again, it can be a strange place.

Several of the volunteers ran over to the lot, and there was a man laying there, gray, with no pulse. He had white foam around his mouth.

Someone dialed 911 and one of the guys, Tom, started CPR. I carry Narcan - which turns off opioid receptors in the nervous system and can reverse an overdose - on me for this very reason. It comes in a nasal spray applicator.

We squirted the Narcan into his nostrils and continued with chest compressions, and after several minutes, we felt a faint pulse.

We kept on with the CPR, then an ambulance arrived. It seemed to take forever for them to get there, but it couldn't have been more than 15 minutes. The EMTs loaded the man into the ambulance, and carted him off to the hospital. He was alive when he left and I pray he is still alive and has found Jesus Christ and changed his life, but I've never seen him again.

The next week two bodies were found nearby, along Chartiers Creek, a small river that runs along the edge of town. They were in body bags.

How does that happen? Again, it's a strange, broken place.

Shorty after the bodies were found, a dismembered woman's body was found in a refrigerator in a hallway of a low-income building a half mile away.

These evil actions and ugly things occur often in McKees Rocks, the poor town where Faithbridge Community Church is located. The community is numb to violence and death and barely reacts when lives are lost in this dangerous environment.

The man hauled off in the ambulance after overdosing was lying dead for a good while. At least twenty minutes before we even got to him. All of the guys from the Good News Place not actively administering first aid were praying intensely while CPR and Narcan were given. I have no doubt it was because of the prayers that we reached a pulse.

We returned to the storefront for the men's bible study, but I was discombobulated - again, I didn't grow up around this kind of stuff - so, unable to concentrate, I stepped outside. I looked up and saw Jesus on the clouds! It wasn't just an image of Him in the sky, it was a personal thing. I could see Him looking directly at me, wearing a dark blue robe. His long locks of hair were waving, blown by the wind up there. His hands were again stretched out to me.

My spirit was thrilled to see Him. He is beautiful and somehow His beauty exudes intense amounts of grace and love. As I watched, he faded from the sky, and I went back inside.

That evening, as the study wrapped up. I went to my bible and started researching the color blue, if it had any biblical significance. I naturally would have associated Jesus with purple or white, as I had seen before. Those colors carry connotations of royalty and holiness, the color of nobility and the sacred biblical priesthood.

My research showed the color blue represents "the Heavens and the Word of God." As I read that, I thanked Jesus for showing me Himself on the clouds. This vision reminded me to stay immersed in God's word, and I do even more now than I did prior - and I was pretty immersed in it then!

Shortly after we closed up the Good News Place for the night, I went up the road to the Worship Center. I went into the church and I told Hogan and our friend Sam Miller, the minister who started the Good News Place about the day.

I explained what happened with the man overdosing, then told them that I saw Jesus on the clouds wearing a blue robe, which means the heavens and the Word of God.

Hogan and my friend Sam Miller both have experienced visions, and Sam said, "The robe must have been purple, for Jesus's royalty."

Right then and there Jesus showed me the vision on the clouds again in a blue robe! I laughed, knowing that Jesus reconfirmed the color of the robe to me, thrilled that my interactions with Him were becoming so frequent and pointed. Jesus *is* royalty, *and* He wants us to stay grounded in His word, for it it God's revelation of Himself for us!

Jesus said to him, "I am the way, the truth, and the life. No one comes to the Father except through Me. ~**John 14:6**

These are the Words of Jesus Christ. He makes it plain that all must have a personal relationship with Him in order to make it to Heaven. We find the keys to doing so in God's holy word. It informs the rest of our walk with Him, from enriching our understanding who God is, to showing us how God wants us to treat others, how we're to pray to God and worship, serving others, discipling folks and loving people in the hopes that they may come to know God.

CHAPTER TWENTY-EIGHT

VISIONS OF HELL

One day I was visiting a friend who'd lost his son many years ago, when his son was 21. He and his son were having difficulties over some reckless behaviors his boy had gotten involved with alongside his fellow construction workers resulting in his son's driver's license being restricted after a DUI.

His son, who lived several towns away, balked at his father's corrective conversations, and had stopped taking his phone calls.

One day the phone rang and it was the police. His son had been killed in an industrial accident with a crane on a job site, struck by a girder when the crane's clutch had given out. The news was shattering.

My friend, who I love dearly and hate to see suffer, continues in the depths of grief as if the accident just happened, even though many, many years have passed.

I understand that for parents, losing a child is

something I can't (thankfully) understand, but it must be a horrid, gutting thing to go through.

I do know other parents, however, whose grief at the loss of a child has been more healthy, allowing them to miss their child, cherish the memories, yet move forward in life. But the mourning has taken control of my friend's life. In a very real way, grief has become his defining characteristic. He can't move on.

Regrets abound. Scenarios play out in his head, leaving him with a lot of I-wish-I-would-have-done thoughts that beat him up, even though he knows that God knows the number of all of our days, and we neither have a time machine nor could have actually changed the outcome.

We've spoken many times about his need to accept Christ, that Jesus can heal him and lift him from misery, but, having read up on similar situations, I think he's tied to his grief by guilt, feeling it would be wrong for him to have any real happiness with his son decades in the grave, unable to have his own happiness here on Earth.

But guilt like that isn't of God. It's an attack, a trap from the demon called *pain*.

> Be anxious for nothing, but in everything by prayer and supplication, with thanksgiving, let your requests be made known to God; [7] and the peace of God,

which surpasses all understanding, will guard your hearts and minds through Christ. ~ **Philippians 4:6-7**

One day, tired of seeing him suffer, knowing that Jesus can improve his situation, I visited my friend to talk about salvation. In a moment of vulnerability, he stated that if his son was in Hell - he'd never shared the hope of salvation with his boy, and didn't believe his ex-wife, who'd never to his knowledge attended any kind of church, had - he couldn't leave him there alone.

Sometimes visions from God can be wonderful. Other times, they can be awful. After my friend said that, an anointing fell upon me and God showed me this:

The son, bloody and battered, was tied to a wooden chair. Blood ran down his face from his scalp, and ran down his arms and legs as he screamed his father's name, crying out in pain for him. Recrimination and a searing, pointed anger raged in his eyes and resounded in his voice.

I could see my friend behind glass, looking at his son, crying hysterically and screaming his boy's name. The son didn't appear to be able to hear his dad or see him, but my friend could see and hear it all. It was a terrible thing, shocking and so upsetting it made me feel sick.

The pain and suffering I witnessed hurt me deeply. The gouging pain I now feel for my friend and his son cannot be explained in any way that conveys its weight. Seeing his son in hell this way was brutal and convicting. We get one run on this Earth, and it's incumbent upon the church to share the gospel because if the opportunity for salvation is missed and the clock runs out, it's for eternity.

I haven't told my friend about this vision, and, to be honest, I hope God allows me to never share it with him. He's barely living as it is, and the brutality of this vision could be the reason to quit living altogether.

I haven't given up on him, and don't plan to. We get together for a meal or some time at car shows here and there. I was pleasantly surprised to hear he now sporadically attends a church down his way, south of here. And I keep praying.

CHAPTER TWENTY-NINE

THE DEVIL AND HIS DEMONS

The Lord continued to give my spirit knowledge and guidance in situations. One time I was at my house, so angry over the chaos and constant sin I see around me, I yelled at the devil, "I hate you devil!"

Suddenly seven figures were standing in a line in front of me. Their faces were metallic, silverish. I'd seen this before in the dreams I had as a child in grade school where I was alone and they were dressed as Nazis, chasing me.

The demons were head-to-toe in this metallic silver. Sort of like the face of the Tin Man in the old Wizard of Oz movie. They were with the devil himself, meaning they must be very important in their dark realm. The devil himself stood dead center, three demons on each side. They stood at perfect, rigid military attention, not moving even when he walked out from their center and turned his eyes towards me.

Deep bulging dark blue veins popped out of his face alongside his prominent nose, his silver hair slicked back. His solid black eyes glared at me, and I could see blood pumping through the arteries on his face. From his slicked hair, protruded two tan, ringed horns, sloping back along his head, almost hidden in the hair. The horns were the same exact complex serpent skin color as the snakes I'd seen so many times in my dreams as a kid, spotted lightly with dull yellows, browns and black.

The veins on his face bulged as if ready to burst with the anger and hatred directed at me with his countenance. He was obviously extremely mad at me. He tried to have me all these years, but had lost me to Jesus and I walk in Christ now, sealed forever by God's Holy Spirit, so he hates me, all that I am, and what I stand for. I love Jesus and will serve Him for all time!

CHAPTER THIRTY

ABORTION

God next gave me a vision of warning about abortion. I know it's a hot button political issue, and some readers might cringe or be angered by this, but I can't help that. I'm calling balls and strikes here, saying what God has shown me.

I was watching a preacher on CBN, and when that ended, the news came on. On the screen appeared a story about a DC bureaucrat serving under the president. He was holding a press conference.

A woman, a lifelong member of his party, and a wealthy executive who'd supported their candidates for years, asked him "What about those among us who are pro-life? Where do we stand? Do we have any place in our party anymore?"

His answer was, "If you are not in support of a woman's right to choose, I'd say there is no room for you in this party."

The camera showed the woman's response as

anger and exasperation flashed on her face. She was shocked.

I was appalled and mad, looking at the situation from my usual political and moral position. Then I heard a quiet voice, one I had never heard before. Soft and high pitched, feminine in tone, the character of it conversational and concerned, as if I were overhearing someone else's interaction.

"What is going to happen to them?" the voice asked.

The strong, deep, emphatic voice of God our Father answered, saying, "Abortion! Over and over again! Arms and limbs!" Then again, "Abortion! Over and over again! Arms and limbs!"

God's wrathful anger dripped from His words. It shook me.

Then God showed me Hell again. In this vision there was an extrusion machine. I am familiar with these machines from industry. What you do is you put a raw material into the machine's hopper on one end, and the finished product comes out in the desired shape at the other end.

This machine, however, was bigger than any extrusion machine I'd ever seen, with tubes that reminded me of the slides at indoor water parks. One large tube fed into the mechanism, then into a smaller tube, then another to a smaller tube, and so on reducing the raw material.

As I looked, God showed me that man again, this

baby murder supporting bureaucrat, in Hell. All around the machine was foul and dark, vacant except for the machine, which roared with the horrid sounds of sawing and grinding.

The man entered the wide side of the machine and exited from the small end, his arms and legs severed and gone. His screams of pain were so loud they drowned out the roaring machine itself.

As I watched, horrified, his arms and legs popped back out from his torso, and he went back again into the machine, coming out again without arms and legs! Over and over again, in an endless cycle of mechanical dismemberment, total violence. I've seen the gruesome pictures of dismembered babies, pulled apart by so-called doctors because they're near full term, ready to be born when the decision is made to kill them.

Some people think Hell is run by the devil, that it will be a place of rebellion and partying. It won't. It's run by God, who kicked the rebellious angels out of Heaven because they challenged His glory and authority. When I saw this vision, I understood just how much the killing of innocent babies angers and offends God.

Horrified and contemplating what I'd been shown, I heard God speak again.

"Tell (one of my siblings) if they ever want to see their child, whom I've brought home and is here with me, again, 'Do not glorify the death of my children with your vote!'"

I committed there and then to tell them, knowing that it would be difficult. God then showed me my precious nephew who had died at the age of eleven, standing in a dark robe with his hands raised in praise to the bright, glorious light emanating from God. My nephew was smiling, as happy as could be. He turned and looked at me with the most loving, beautiful and peaceful smile I have ever had cast my way from anyone, anywhere. It was divine, holy, amazing.

God spoke again, telling me that the children are His diamonds, His gems, precious to Him. His voice was steeped in sadness at babies being rejected, killed in their innocence for the crime of merely existing. I could see diamonds floating from the Earth to Heaven, thousands and thousands of them and I was overcome with this sadness.

They were beautiful and pure like I had never seen before. Each gem sparkled brightly. Hundreds of thousands of gems, babies murdered by abortion and other callous murderous acts. It was a constant stream of diamond babies going to heaven, like an upward, slow motion meteor shower.

I cannot emphasize the anger our Creator has at us taking on the authority to kill, playing god ourselves, killing over petty, selfish reasons. God alone is the

Author and Finisher of life… and He is not pleased at our usurpation.

I was extremely sad after experiencing this vision. They can be brutally heavy, but are for God's purposes. All of them, pleasant, wondrous or painful and horrifying are mind blowing, supernatural.

It's no wonder people think only troubled people have visions. Most folks have no point of reference for things outside the bounds of nature, and struggle to believe or understand. Combine that with the fact that folks are mostly wed to what they already believe and uninterested in being informed that they are in error or morally wrong.

That makes visions tough for folks, but necessary for God. If merely putting His standards and truths in His revelation of Himself through the holy word were enough to prevent people from building false beliefs and surrounding them with justifications and excuses to hold them up, visions and prophecy wouldn't likely be a necessary tool for Him.

I will never believe another person's claim of visions unless I can align it with God's word. The bible is the ultimate authority and cuts through the chaff. A lot of claimed visions are emotionally driven thoughts, imaginative aspersions or hallucinations, and not from God. Others are mere demonic trickery meant to mislead.

Believe me, however, when Heaven speaks, you know it, and you can verify it perfectly with scripture.

My sheep hear My voice, and I know them, and they follow Me. [28] And I give them eternal life, and they shall never perish; neither shall anyone snatch them out of My hand. ~**John 10:27-28**

CHAPTER THIRTY- ONE

THE MEETING

I met with Pastor Hogan about this vision, troubled about how to tell my sibling what God had said. I love my family and don't want to hurt them.

I was extremely upset, partly because I know we don't think alike so I try to stay away from political discussions, but this, to God, is not political. It is breaking a commandment. "Thou shall not murder".

I knew my sibling's beliefs were pro-life. They had attended rallies in support of life in D.C., and stood appalled at the thought of killing a developing baby. But their belief didn't make it into the voting booth, so, because they supported other things a candidate might be for, they would vote for abortion.

It took me three days to get the courage to talk to members of my family about what God had shown me and said.

I knew it had to be done. That's why I committed to do it on the spot, even if it was taking a few days to act upon. I also wanted to tell them about their son, and the peace and joy I had seen on his face.

So, I prayed hard, real hard. God commanded it, so I prayed for Him to guide it.

That gave me the confidence and courage to see my family, sit down and talk. And God was faithful to guide the conversation and keep peace with us. We shed many tears over their son. I was pleased to be able to tell them their son is with God, and beautiful.

That was great news for them. We cried and cried.

I directed the conversation to as non-political an approach as I could to explain God's stance, but the vote topic had to be addressed because God had directly said so.

In a two-party system, our choices are limited. Pro-life, pro-abortion… or mostly irrelevant. We might want to vote for less government spending and less taxes or for higher taxes on the well-to-do and defunding the police, but in a binary system we're casting a vote in support or opposition to killing babies in utero.

God made it plain that this matter is not ancillary to Him. Vote for abortion and He is not pleased, no matter what euphemisms or outlandish scenarios we conjure to justify it.

Saying "I'm personally against abortion. I'd never kill my own offspring, but I'm 'pro-choice' because it's not my place to tell someone else what to do" is like saying "I'm personally against spousal abuse. I'd never kick the crap out of my wife, but I'm pro-choice on the matter because it's not my place to tell another fella he can't beat the cheese out of his spouse." And God isn't swayed by our mental gymnastics.

I pray my family member voted for the party that stands for life, not abortion, or at the very least didn't vote for candidates who support abortion. To this day I don't know what they did, but I did as God asked.

What scares me the most is the question from the small, gentle voice at the beginning of this vision.

"What is going to happen to them?"

Who is *them?* Just the candidate and his crew, or anyone that votes for the party that supports abortion?

I personally believe the latter, because of how personal God made it when he told me what to tell my sibling.

Murder is murder. His grace is vast and deep, I believe our Creator created us and these babies and in His eyes, they're precious, especially in the innocence inherent before a baby has much agency of its own. His gems, His diamonds.

God has shown me His anger about this and I cannot believe anything less. God is the Author and Finisher of life. Any other view is of this world, not from God.

The Good News is forgiveness

I believe this topic is the main reason God had me write this book.

I wrote earlier that I was involved with an abortion. I was raised to love and cherish life and God and all living beings. My parents were an amazing example of living a decent, moral life.

My heart struggled to get over what I did. I could never forgive myself and I knew I was totally unworthy of Heaven even though I gave my life to Christ for real in my late forties.

At one point I thought the medical challenges I've suffered were my punishment for what I had done and the ungodly life I had lived.

I was so very wrong. I always loved God in concept, and believed in Him… but I never knew Jesus. I grew up Catholic and, at my church they really didn't emphasize the cross and Jesus crucified, but for Eastertime.

It seemed to me to be more about the Virgin Mary and the Saints, who had days dedicated to them throughout the calendar, than Jesus.

When I committed my life to Jesus, my health began to deteriorate at a rapid rate, and I was always seemingly one beat away from death. Due, likely, in large part to this, I drew closer and closer to Jesus. I was dependent on Him for my survival. Regardless, I didn't believe I would make it to Heaven because of abortion, and teaching about "mortal sin" in my childhood church - unredeemable actions, including murder, that the church then taught God would never forgive.

Then Jesus saved me.

I know there are many men and women out there that believed the same thing, thinking they are unworthy to God because of abortion. Jesus Christ died for you and I, sinners, so if we accept Him as our Savior and repent, we will be forgiven.

You have read about my vision when I was on the floor with the picture frame under me as God showed me the taking away of my sins.

I now know that "mortal sin" is a lie. Jesus will forgive any and all sin when someone makes him the Lord of their life. The only "mortal sin" is rejecting Jesus.

Please I beg of you, if you have not accepted Christ to do so while you have time.

So you feel you are unworthy? That's true. Welcome to the club. God's word tells us all us fall short of the glory of God, and that what we earn by our sin is death.

But God made a way with Jesus and the cross. Jesus took our sin upon Himself, and killed it off on the cross. In Him and His resurrection from the dead we find eternal life.

Mercy is not getting what we deserve. That's the cross.

Grace is gaining what we don't deserve. That's the resurrection.

But we have to receive and embrace the gift while this life persists. If you wait until you die, it is too late.

Please hear my words. I beg of you to call on Jesus. He will forgive you and show you His love and peace for you.

> For the wages of sin *is* death, but the gift of God *is* eternal life in Christ Jesus our Lord. ~**Romans 6:23**

CHAPTER THIRTY-TWO

BABY CORPSES AS A COMMODITY

One day I was watching CBN news and they were talking about organizations that are taking aborted babies and selling their body parts or using them for experiments in lab environments.

The University of Pittsburgh was caught doing exactly that, and it sickened me. They are a major employer in our area, a giant, multi-hospital conglomerate that trains up physicians, techs and nurses.

This gruesome transaction happens all around the world, increasing the demand for abortion as entities want the tissue. They will have to face God, our Creator, on their day of judgment.

While the news was discussing this disgusting topic, they showed video of people selling parts using a catalog, like a menu. This price for a liver, that price for a voicebox, etc. In the video, some of the "vendors" were eating while talking about selling baby parts. Downright evil.

While watching this, I fell into the spirit again. As I sat on my couch, the Lord screamed:

"They have turned dead babies into a commodity!" The whole Earth appeared in front of me as if I was watching from space, and a stock exchange ticker tape encircled the world showing dead babies on the stock exchange! God was furious.

God changed my viewing angle and I could see myself, and the curvature of the Earth. Massive, thick dark clouds started rolling over the entire globe, completely enveloping the Earth.

Then God spoke in the face of the darkness and evil.

"Hold on to Me and stay strong!" He said.

This vision recurs for me over and over again as the world comes closer to its eventual end. I'll speak of it again later.

The other day I was with Pastor Hogan and the news reported on Canada's own dead baby market. I got sick and the exact vision occurred to me again.

I have deep concern about this vision. The entire Earth covered in dark clouds, representing evil, foreshadowing desperate end times, destruction, and suffering.

God's anger about our turning away from Him is real. Abortion and the cultural abandonment of plain truths are an affront to Him. He defines truth in all

He has made, declared and sustains. This vision is a warning to us of what will take place. The followers of folly, embracers of evil, and those who champion the killing of innocents will clearly answer to God.

CHAPTER THIRTY-THREE

THE LAST SUPPER TABLE

That winter our church worship team was invited to a prayer meeting at another church. A few of us attended. It was a very snowy night, which kept attendance down, and it was in a rural area, the next county over. Around 30 people were there all together.

The agenda started with prayer, then our band led worship. After the music, more prayer, then the Lord's Supper, and we would close in prayer.

I was sitting on the riser behind my drum set, and people were queuing straight in directly in front of me to receive communion. Pastor Hogan was in pain due to recurring medical issues he deals with, and had laid back onto the riser.

The worship team had been gently playing some instrumental music, and wound that down so they could receive communion, too. I leaned forward to stand and get communion when I saw Jesus seated at the table breaking bread!

This time Jesus's hair was shorter, and he was breaking off sections of the unleavened bread to hand out. He seemed to note me noticing Him, stopped, turned His head toward me, and smiled. This close, I could clearly see His eyes, better than the other times, and they were so bright, so blue. I smiled, amazed and His smile shone back like the sun, warming my soul on this blustery, cold day.

I could see people at the table, but I was clearly focused on Jesus. They seemed to be fellowshipping with Jesus, wearing red, blue and white robes, but each unique to its wearer. Most of them had long hair, which harkened back to old paintings of the Last Supper, and made me feel at home, having come from the world of musicians where such style is common. It was beautiful: Jesus breaking bread with saints or angels while we were breaking bread in His name, as He commanded down through the ages. How cool is that?

I knew from this vision that Jesus was delighted with us on that snowy night. Praising and worshiping our Savior regardless of the weather. Regardless of the time or season. Even writing about this brings back the warm feeling of God's approval that night and refreshes my soul.

It was beautiful. No, beyond beauty. Perfection. I've never looked at the Lord's Supper the same. Communion indeed! Truly having communion with Jesus Himself!

For as often as you eat this bread and drink this cup, you proclaim the Lord's death till He comes ~1 **Corinthians 11:26**

And as they were eating, Jesus took bread, blessed and broke *it,* and gave *it* to the disciples and said, "Take, eat; this is My body." Then He took the cup, and gave thanks, and gave *it* to them, saying, "Drink from it, all of you. [28] For this is My blood of the new covenant, which is shed for many for the remission of sins. ~**Matthew 26: 26-28**

But I say to you, I will not drink of this fruit of the vine from now on until that day when I drink it new with you in My Father's kingdom." ~**Matthew 26:29**

Then Jesus said to them, "Most assuredly, I say to you, unless you eat the flesh of the Son of Man and drink His blood, you have no life in you. [54] Whoever eats My flesh and drinks My blood has eternal life, and I will raise him up at the last day. [55] For My flesh is food indeed, and My blood is drink indeed. [56] He who eats My flesh and drinks My blood abides in Me, and I in him. [57]

As the living Father sent Me, and I live because of the Father, so he who feeds on Me will live because of Me. [58] This is the bread which came down from heaven—not as your fathers ate the manna, and are dead. He who eats this bread will live forever. ~**John 6:53-58**

CHAPTER THIRTY-FOUR

TWO THOUGHTS THAT TROUBLE ME

I've had many visions and words from God but two ideas keep resonating in my own spirit.

One, that Jesus Christ is love. Jesus Christ will forgive all that accept Him as Lord and Savior and repent from sin. Yet, in our society now Jesus is often treated like the unseemly stranger on the side of the road. Cold, starving, and lonely. Forgotten and left behind. His amazing holy words forgotten by much of this world.

So many reject the stranger, focused on themselves, afraid of anything outside of their circle, not seeing that it is He that can help them. So they make a wide berth instead of reaching out to Him.

This harms them in many ways, including them never learning how to embrace God's love and share it with the stranger, the person different than them, the one they judge without cause.

Therefore love the stranger, for you were strangers in the land of Egypt. **~Deuteronomy 10:19**

The stranger who dwells among you shall be to you as one born among you, and you shall love him as yourself; for you were strangers in the land of Egypt: I *am* the LORD your God. **~Leviticus 19:34**

For the LORD will have mercy on Jacob, and will still choose Israel, and settle them in their own land. The strangers will be joined with them, and they will cling to the house of Jacob. **~Isaiah 14:1**

"You have heard that it was said, 'You shall love your neighbor and hate your enemy.' [44] But I say to you, love your enemies, bless those who curse you, do good to those who hate you, and pray for those who spitefully use you and persecute you, **~Matthew 5:43-44**

And the King will answer and say to them, 'Assuredly, I say to you, inasmuch as you did *it* to one of the least of these My brethren, you did *it* to Me. **~Matthew 25:40**

Beloved, you do faithfully whatever you do for the brethren and for strangers, ⁶who have borne witness of your love before the church. *If* you send them forward on their journey in a manner worthy of God, you will do well, ⁷because they went forth for His name's sake, taking nothing from the Gentiles. ⁸We therefore ought to receive such, that we may become fellow workers for the truth. ~3 **John 1: 5-8**

Let brotherly love continue. ²Do not forget to entertain strangers, for by so *doing* some have unwittingly entertained angels. ³Remember the prisoners as if chained with them—those who are mistreated—since you yourselves are in the body also.⁴Marriage *is* honorable among all, and the bed undefiled; but fornicators and adulterers God will judge.⁵ *Let your* conduct *be* without covetousness; *be* content with such things as you have. For He Himself has said, "I will never leave you nor forsake you." ⁶So we may boldly say: "The LORD *is* my helper; I will not fear. What can man do to me?" ~**Hebrews 13:1-6**

Dear reader, are you that person that ignores others? If you are, I beg of you to repent and open yourself up to others! They are God's cherished beings, created in His image and they matter.

This world is falling apart because of individual self-centeredness, which leads to corruption.

The families are broken, churches are closing, and many struggling to stay open have misguidedly patterned themselves after the world and no longer speak the truth about God's word. They bend it and twist it to fit today's culture and society, appealing to the same self-centeredness and arrogant assuredness that brought about the spiraling corruption all around us.

Even government, that bastion of self promotion and abuse piles on by trading federal grants and money to ministries in exchange for promises that churches will not teach the totality of God's word but leave out that of which our soiled culture disapproves. This is horrible. It may seem unkind to hear that something one prefers is a sin in God's eyes, but only in the manner that a cancer diagnosis from your doctor seems unkind. It hurts, but without it, you miss the truth and won't ever pursue the cure. God does not change. He is eternal. The same when He revealed Himself through the word as He is now and will be for all time.

The second very strong feeling that troubles me since I started receiving these divine images is that the world has turned against God.

Here in the United States, where, in its early years the French observer and philosopher Alexis de Tocqueville saw how America's liberty was informed and fueled by its faith, he wrote "America is great because she is good."

Now we're far from great, because we're far from good as a country. Far from good because, while our "leaders" pay lip service to God, we're far from Him. We call his designed biology wrong. His moral standards immoral and bigoted. The boundaries He gives us to enable freedom without anarchic collapse have been claimed shackling and unfair, and when we institute policies abandoning them and find chaos, we claim He must not love us to allow the chaos.

God is the Righteous Judge, and even more than that, He is right. His ways work. His word is the owner's manual to life, written by life's Author.

In the end there will be judgment for those who have rejected God. Those without Christ will not be judged by God's rejection of them, but their rejection of Him.

If you are confused whether this nation started as a Christian nation, read the "Mayflower Compact" from the pilgrims below. They came seeking freedom to worship God, to settle in peace with one another and with God. Surely, others came later who were not focused so, looking to exploit the land and seek riches in a land yet to have laws and civil authorities across vast stretches of the continent, but they weren't the original migrators, nor did their mindset make up the majority of the nation's founders at the time of the Constitution's adoption.

The Mayflower Compact Agreement between the Settlers at New Plymouth, 1620

In the name of God, Amen. We whose names are underwritten, the loyal Subjects of our dread sovereign Lord King James, by the grace of God of Great Britain, France, and Ireland King, Defender of the Faith, &c. Having undertaken for the glory of God, and advancement of the Christian Faith, and honor of our King and Country, a Voyage to plant the first Colony in the Northern parts of Virginia; do by these presents solemnly and mutually, in the presence of God and one another, covenant, and combine ourselves together into a civil body politick, for our better ordering and preservation and furtherance of the ends aforesaid; and by virtue hereof do enact, constitute, and frame such just and equal Laws, Ordinances, acts, constitutions, and offices from time to time, as shall be thought most meet and convenient for the general good of the Colony; unto which we promise all due submission and obedience. In witness whereof we have hereunto subscribed our names at Cape Cod the 11. of November, in the year of the reign of our sovereign Lord King James, of England,

France, and Ireland, the eighteenth, and of Scotland the fifty-fourth, Anno Domini 1620.

John Carver, William Bradford, Edward Winslow, William Brewster, Isaac Allerton, Myles Standish, John Alden, Samuel Fuller, Christopher Martin, William Mullins, William White, Richard Warren, John Howland, Stephen Hopkins,Edward Tilley, John Tilley,Francis Cooke, Thomas Rogers, Thomas Tinker, John Rigsdale, Edward Fuller, John Turner, Francis Eaton, James Chilton, John Crackstone, John Billington, Moses Fletcher, John Goodman, Degory Priest, Thomas Williams, Gilbert Winslow, Edmund Margesson, Peter Browne, Richard Britteridge, George Soule, Richard Clarke, Richard Gardiner, John Allerton, Thomas English, Edward Doty, Edward Leister

This second concern includes the coming of the end of times. The final days. I don't know when the end is, but this world is rapidly pulling away from God - exactly as the bible states the world will!

If you know the bible you cannot reject the biblical prophecies that foretold of this time. Jesus stated there will be signs, and it's hard to argue that the signs aren't here now.

CHAPTER THIRTY-FIVE

THE DEMONIC POLITICIAN

Sitting in my living room after another day in the studio, watching CBN news, there he was again, speaking against people who are Pro-life, reiterating his stance that there is no room in his party for those opposed to abortion!

I heard God's voice, strong and deep. The powerful voice of authority, direct and to the point. His voice commands attention, instantly blocking out all outside voices or noises, aligning my spirit with the Holy Spirit. Sometimes I sense myself transported to another time or place. Other times, my immediate surroundings fade as I'm pulled into a sort of tunnel vision, focusing solely where He wants my attention in the here and now.

God said, "It's him." When He first said it, I had no way to understand. That's why God took me on a journey back through my life and showed me all the attacks through which I'd come, carried by Him from my earliest days, protecting me from the devil's demon set to take me out.

In some way, the same demon assigned to trouble me throughout the decades has inhabited this man. I guess it makes sense that for some reason he, and he alone, stands out as particularly evil whenever I see his visage, despite his generally cherubic, unthreatening look. I sense in him the same predatory presence my own spirit has been reacting to, terrified and harassed by for years and years.

The bureaucrat, now working for the current administration in DC, is no longer the human born to his parents decades ago. The battle, for him, was lost years ago, and his soul subjugated. If that poor soul lives within him at all, it lives trapped, subjected to the very same demon that wanted to do the same to me throughout my years, or worse.

It resonates from Him, creating some weird connection or recognition within my spirit, a heightened sense of danger, like a puppy reacts when its abuser walks through the door. I couldn't grasp it fully until God plainly stated it. His is the same demon that showed up, attacking me in my house when I became deathly ill. The same demon I would awaken to feeling sick and terribly afraid from nightmares, who would be inches from my face as my eyes opened.

Again, being raised in a benign, seemingly powerless, ritualistic church, all of this was not just unknown, but unknowable to me. The limits I myself placed on spiritual understanding out of misguided surety and fear of the fantastic had also hindered me.

When I would hear a charismatic Christian talk of "devil assignments" and such, I would dismiss it as folly - even though I'd suffered from it all my years!

This demon had an evil commission,charged by the devil to ruin my life, to kill me if he could. To trash my livelihood, destroy my marriage and was there for all of the tragedies and near-death crises I survived by God's grace and protection. He and others of his ilk desire to kill this country and all of western, liberty-embracing, faith permitting culture by tearing down the very pillars placed by God - the person, the family, the school, industry, the church, and the civil governments dedicated to enabling freedom - and turning people away from God with confusion and lies.

I won't say the bureaucrat's name because I'm not a lawyer and don't know the liability that could put me at risk with, but - even as some will see this as silly or crazy - many, I know, will feel the truth of this resonate with their spirit.

We don't think about oppression and possession, and as many have said over the years, "the devil's greatest trick was convincing the world he doesn't exist," but I expect worldly backlash to come down on me like a hammer for stating it.

It doesn't matter to me.

I have to speak the truths that God has shown me. Make this clear: I'm not sharing a political opinion or statement here, this was from God!

Evil isn't exclusive to one particular faction or party, as it resides in the hearts of mankind, but the Lord has shown that as this possessed person has risen through the ranks, his power to influence and spoil the whole organization grows, giving the devil more and more power within, resulting in more and more evil and corruption of our institutions. This man is *an* anti-christ. Perhaps not *the* anti-christ of end times eschatological theology, but one of its ilk, for sure.

I know the weight of these statements. I care not about man's judgment of me, but If I were to make false statements about what I have seen, experienced and heard, the consequences - which certainly matter to me - would be horrific. One falsely claiming prophecy in the Old Testament was condemned by God to be killed for it. In the New Testament, Jesus stated the price for "misleading these little ones and causing them to stumble" would be worse than having a millstone hung around one's neck and being tossed into the depths of the ocean.

My home and citizenship is in Heaven. I would not dare risk that by lying about what God has shown me.

For such *are* false apostles, deceitful workers, transforming themselves into apostles of Christ. [14] And no wonder! For the devil himself transforms himself into an angel of light. [15] Therefore *it is* no great thing if his ministers also transform themselves into ministers of righteousness, whose end will be according to their works. ~**2 Corinthians 11:13-15**

When you have a vision, you know it. God stops your world completely. There is no wondering or questioning of its veracity, other than working out the purpose of the vision itself.

I do not watch the so-called "prophets" on tv or YouTube because the few I have seen are so obviously charlatans, claiming self-serving, self-enriching things, and making claims debunked by God's word itself. God didn't reveal Himself to us through His holy word to go around individually telling people things about Himself contrary to His revelation and out of character.

CHAPTER THIRTY-SIX

WHAT ARE THE SIGNS?

Dr. David Jeremiah, famed theologian and California pastor, listed the signs God told us to watch for.

1. **Deception**: *Jesus stated in the end times there will be an increasing danger of deception. More and more people don't trust our government because of its actions against the American people. The main network news stations have all become propaganda mills, slanting stories, outright lying and notorious for hiding the truth. Our own public-school systems are hiding troubling things about students from their parents in many cases.*

> And Jesus answered and said to them: "Take heed that no one deceives you. [5] For many will come in My name, saying, 'I am the Christ,' and will deceive many.
> **~Matthew 24:4-5**

For such *are* false apostles, deceitful workers, transforming themselves into apostles of Christ. [14] And no wonder! For the devil himself transforms himself into an angel of light. [15] Therefore *it is* no great thing if his ministers also transform themselves into ministers of righteousness, whose end will be according to their works. ~**2 Corinthians 11:13-15**

But know this, that in the last days perilous times will come: [2] For men will be lovers of themselves, lovers of money, boasters, proud, blasphemers, disobedient to parents, unthankful, unholy, [3] unloving, unforgiving, slanderers, without self-control, brutal, despisers of good, [4] traitors, headstrong, haughty, lovers of pleasure rather than lovers of God, [5] having a form of godliness but denying its power. And from such people turn away! ~**2 Timothy 3:1-5**

Now the Spirit expressly says that in latter times some will depart from the faith, giving heed to deceiving spirits and doctrines of demons, ~**1 Timothy 4:1**

> For false christs and false prophets will rise and show great signs and wonders to deceive, if possible, even the elect.
> **~Matthew 24:24**

> For the time will come when they will not endure sound doctrine, but according to their own desires, *because* they have itching ears, they will heap up for themselves teachers; ⁴ and they will turn *their* ears away from the truth, and be turned aside to fables. **~2 Timothy 4:3-4**

2. The sign of disputes among the nations *Nations are warring now, and the divide has spread into the streets of nations not yet involved, inching us closer to what the bible says will be war among all nations. Look at Israel, God's chosen land and people, subject to hatred and massacre century after century. The world is aligning Israel just as the bible states even as I write, and despite the United States being bound by treaty to support them in their defense, our current leaders are waffling in support and the International Court in the Hague is threatening to arrest Israel's leaders for defending themselves militarily after a Hamas attack slaughtered 1200 Jewish civilians. The people of the world are harming Jews, and helping or supporting terrorists.*

And you will hear of wars and rumors of wars. See that you are not troubled; for all *these things* must come to pass, but the end is not yet. [7] For nation will rise against nation, and kingdom against kingdom. And there will be famines, pestilences, and earthquakes in various places. [8] All these *are* the beginning of sorrows. [9] "Then they will deliver you up to tribulation and kill you, and you will be hated by all nations for My name's sake ~**Matthew 24:6-7-8-9**

3.The sign of Devastation *Hunger and starvation are worldwide now. You can't turn on the TV without ads begging for help for the poor, the hungry or those in need of shelter. It is becoming more and more prevalent in the United States as prices have skyrocketed on commodities, impacting families horribly. Homeless people are everywhere, tent cities across the land. People are murdering for food, for survival. Drugs and alcohol run rampant and addiction is crippling vast sectors of the populace - and it looks like that is exactly what the government wants to create dependence on them instead of the liberty of independent ability to survive.*

For nation will rise against nation, and kingdom against kingdom. And there will be famines, pestilences, and earthquakes in various places ~**Matthew 24:7**

His power shall be mighty, but not by his
own power;
He shall destroy fearfully,
And shall prosper and thrive;
He shall destroy the mighty, and *also* the
holy people. **~Daniel 8:24**

4.The sign of deliverance into tribulation Quoting
Dr Jeremiah, *"In the last days there will be an explosion of
antagonism towards God's people. Christians are murdered
for their faith daily around the world. Many countries would
kill you immediately for Christianity. The entire world as we
once knew it is turning against Israel.*

> "Then they will deliver you up to
> tribulation and kill you, and you will be
> hated by all nations for My name's sake.
> **~Matthew 24:9**

> Therefore judge nothing before the time,
> until the Lord comes, who will both bring
> to light the hidden things of darkness and
> reveal the counsels of the hearts. Then
> each one's praise will come from God. **~1
> Corinthians 4:5**

> Little children, it is the last hour; and
> as you have heard that the Antichrist is
> coming, even now many antichrists have

come, by which we know that it is the last hour. ¹⁹ They went out from us, but they were not of us; for if they had been of us, they would have continued with us; but *they went out* that they might be made manifest, that none of them were of us.~1 **John 2:18**

This is the will of the Father who sent Me, that of all He has given Me I should lose nothing, but should raise it up at the last day ~**John 6:39**

Now a certain ruler asked Him, saying, "Good Teacher, what shall I do to inherit eternal life?" ¹⁹So Jesus said to him, "Why do you call Me good? No one *is* good but One, *that is,* God. ²⁰ You know the commandments: 'Do not commit adultery,' 'Do not murder,' 'Do not steal,' 'Do not bear false witness,' 'Honor your father and your mother.' "²¹ And he said, "All these things I have kept from my youth."²² So when Jesus heard these things, He said to him, "You still lack one thing. Sell all that you have and distribute to the poor, and you will have treasure in heaven; and come, follow Me."²³ But when he heard this, he became very sorrowful, for he was very rich. ~**Luke 18:18-23**

But the cowardly, unbelieving, abominable, murderers, sexually immoral, sorcerers, idolaters, and all liars shall have their part in the lake which burns with fire and brimstone, which is the second death. ~**Revelation 21:8**

Now the Spirit expressly says that in latter times some will depart from the faith, giving heed to deceiving spirits and doctrines of demons, ² speaking lies in hypocrisy, having their own conscience seared with a hot iron, ³ forbidding to marry, *and commanding* to abstain from foods which God created to be received with thanksgiving by those who believe and know the truth. ⁴ For every creature of God *is* good, and nothing is to be refused if it is received with thanksgiving; ⁵ for it is sanctified by the word of God and prayer. ~**1 Timothy 4:1-5**

CHAPTER THIRTY-SEVEN

THE HOLY SPIRIT SAVES ME AGAIN

Recently, I was in the hospital for pancreatitis. They did surgery and the doctors had removed my gallbladder to relieve pressure on the pancreas.

I have been hospitalized so many times before that I knew the operating room nurses there with the doctors who had helped me before.

Pittsburgh is not tiny town in the middle of nowhere, and the UPMC organization has more than ten thousand employees, yet I'm so familiar to them that my friends joke they'll name a hospital after me.

I have been suffering from pancreatitis for a long while and it had hospitalized me several times before this visit. The condition is very painful at times, and troubles me at least part of each day.

The procedure went well, the doctors affirmed. However, I was put on a feeding tube to go home with after a month in the hospital.

I stopped by the church on my way home to say hi, then went home.

At home I began to feel nauseous and pain rose up in my gut. I wasn't right, but I was recovering from surgery, so I figured it was par for the course and I'd just have to suck it up for a while. I took a pain pill to calm my raging gut, and I fell asleep. This pain went on for several days.

A week later I stopped by the 7/11 to get a coffee on the way to the church. I picked up what I needed, but dropped a dollar bill on the floor. As I bent down to get it, I became very dizzy and my thoughts became all jumbled. I turned back to the folks at the counter and said "Call an ambulance, " then fell to the ground.

The staff there helped me up and I asked them to help me get to my car to sit and wait for the ambulance. I was going in and out of consciousness. The store manager, a lovely Christian woman I see most days, stayed and prayed with me. Praise the Lord for faithful people.

The ambulance came and I was placed on a stretcher and loaded in. I told the driver I needed to go to UPMC Presby, but they said I needed to go to the nearest hospital. I argued, explaining, as much as I could, that all of my care had to be at Presby because of my myriad issues, and they finally agreed to take me there.

I kept floating going in and out of consciousness and

I became very cold, freezing so bad that they had to hold me still from the shaking. I was in shock. I barely remember the ride to the hospital but the EMT's later told me I almost didn't make it.

I arrived at the E.R. and was put into a room. They hooked me up to the machines, and noticed my body temperature, blood pressure, and heart rate were extremely low.

They quickly pushed me into the CT scan room. They shoved me to the front of the line, in front of all of the waiting patients in the small waiting area, and lifted me into the machine, telling the tech it was an emergency.. I could barely breathe and my chest hurt so bad. I was still freezing, even under heating pads and blankets. I was totally confused and disoriented.

Throughout all of this time I prayed, asking Jesus to save me.

I could feel the Holy Spirit all about me, like the Spirit was holding me up, supporting me. Any thought of dying fled right then. God had me.

The Holy Spirit kept me alive. I was rushed into surgery as soon as the results of the CT scan came through.

I had never healed from the gallbladder surgery. I was bleeding internally.

The doctors found 2 1/2 liters of blood in my abdominal cavity. My gut was floating in blood. Once more I'd been brought close to death's door, and no doubt the devil was near, rooting for my demise... but God saved me again!

These difficult physical attacks on my health have really taken a toll on me. The devil knows of this book and has tried again and again to prevent me from writing it.

It's not War and Peace in size, but this short book has taken me three years to write. The devil would tie up my mind with discouragement or distraction, or pound me with illness, then I'd call on Jesus to help me or heal me and He has again and again.

Pastor Hogan witnessed a lot of my suffering and was often the only one there for me. I'm grateful for his friendship.

The Holy Spirit carried me throughout this difficult period. I know this, I felt His presence. Praise the Lord!

CHAPTER THIRTY-EIGHT

ISRAEL UNDER ATTACK

As anyone paying attention knows, war is occurring all around the world, and I believe it will only get worse.

I don't hope for it, but I believe it. I won't claim to know when the end times will happen, but I believe we are at a point that will serve as the beginning of a big downfall. I hate that, because I believe those causing the mess are evil and the folks blindly participating in the destruction serve ideologies that are soiled and fruitless, never able to benefit mankind.

When I saw on television the attack on Israel on 10/7/23, I became extremely sick. My stomach felt like I was punched and my spirit seemed to take the attack by proxy. I found myself bent over, having a hard time breathing for many minutes, until I was finally able to straighten up and breathe.

My spirit hurts for Israel. God's chosen people suffer so many slings and arrows, and most of the young minds that rage against them have no understanding. In the Arab world, children are steeped with hatred of the Jews. On western university campuses, Marxist professors poison soft heads with propaganda, knowing only Marx's prescription for chaos - the tearing down of all solid pillars upon which society is platformed.

The world is turning against God's chosen people. History shows the struggles for Jews from the beginning of time. Constantly displaced from the Holy Land as prisoners, refugees and slaves throughout the Old Testament era. Then, when Rome destroyed Jerusalem 40 years after Christ's resurrection and ascension, the Jewish people were dispersed and displaced until 1948, only given back access to their land as the world stood appalled by what Hitler and his monstrous regime had done to the Jews. I believe as time goes on, things will get worse.

More and more countries are turning against Israel just as the Bible prophesies will happen. Even our own United States, bound by treaty to Israel's defense, is seeing resistance on the streets, shouts of "death to Israel" and lukewarm support from our president. Less than a quarter century after 9/11, and only a few months after the 10/7 attacks in Israel, folks are actively crying out support for terrorists and denouncing God's chosen nation.

'He bows down, he lies down as a lion;
And as a lion, who shall rouse him?'
"Blessed *is* he who blesses you,
And cursed *is* he who curses you."
~Numbers 24:9

I will bless those who bless you (Israel),
And I will curse him who curses you;
And in you all the families of the earth
shall be blessed. **~Genesis 12:3**

Judah *is* a lion's whelp;
From the prey, my son, you have gone up .
He bows down, he lies down as a lion;
And as a lion, who shall rouse him?
~Genesis 49:9

Folks, we are in critical times. If you understand God's word deeply, you will understand what's going on here and around the world. But I do not want you to be ignorant, brethren, concerning those who have fallen asleep, lest you sorrow as others who have no hope. [14] For if we believe that Jesus died and rose again, even so God will bring with Him those who sleep in Jesus. [15] For this we say to you by the word of the Lord, that we who are alive *and* remain until the coming of the Lord will by no means precede those who are asleep. [16] For the Lord Himself will descend from heaven with a shout, with the voice of an archangel, and with the trumpet of God. And the dead in Christ will rise first. [17] Then we who are alive *and* remain shall be caught up together with them in the clouds to meet the Lord in the air. And thus we shall always be with the Lord. [18] Therefore comfort one another with these words. ~**1 Thessalonians 4:13-18**

Behold, I will make Jerusalem a cup of drunkenness to all the surrounding peoples, when they lay siege against Judah and Jerusalem. [3] And it shall happen in that day that I will make Jerusalem a very heavy stone for all peoples; all who would heave it away will surely be cut in pieces, though all nations of the earth are gathered against it. [4] In that day," says the LORD, "I will strike every horse with confusion, and its rider with madness; I will open My eyes on the house of Judah, and will strike every horse of the peoples with blindness ~**Zechariah 12:2-4**

Then two *men* will be in the field: one will be taken and the other left. [41] Two *women will be* grinding at the mill: one will be taken and the other left. ~**Matthew 24: 40-41**

But know this, that in the last days perilous times will come: [2] For men will be lovers of themselves, lovers of money, boasters, proud, blasphemers, disobedient to parents, unthankful, unholy, [3] unloving, unforgiving, slanderers, without self-control, brutal, despisers of good, [4] traitors, headstrong, haughty, lovers of pleasure rather than lovers of God, [5] having a form of godliness but denying its power. And from such people turn away! ~**2 Timothy 3:1-5**

And you will hear of wars and rumors of wars. See that you are not troubled; for all *these things* must come to pass, but the end is not yet ~**Matthew 24:6**

"But of that day and hour no one knows, not even the angels in heaven, nor the Son, but only the Father ~**Mark 13:32**

For nation will rise against nation, and kingdom against kingdom. And there will be famines, pestilences, and earthquakes in various places. ~**Matthew 24:7**

in a moment, in the twinkling of an eye, at the last trumpet. For the trumpet will sound, and the dead will be raised incorruptible, and we shall be changed. [53] For this corruptible must put on incorruption, and this mortal *must* put on immortality. [54] So when this corruptible has put on incorruption, and this mortal has put on immortality, then shall be brought to pass the saying that is written: "Death is swallowed up in victory." ~**1 Corinthians 15:52-54**

CHAPTER THIRTY-NINE

THE NATURAL MAN

If you are a Christian and are persecuted for your faith, that is a blessing, although it rarely feels like one.

The Bible speaks of many difficulties the world will experience in end times. The Bible also speaks about those who mock you. It is very simple, let's let God's word explain;

> But the natural man does not receive the things of the Spirit of God, for they are foolishness to him; nor can he know *them*, because they are spiritually discerned. ~1 **Corinthians 2:14**

"The natural man" here is person without God.

He "does not receive the things of the Spirit of God," that is, God's blessings, healings, words or visions. Miracles, prayers answered, etc.

"For they are foolishness unto them." Without God, he wrongly sees the things of faith as folly.

"Neither can he know them," or gain an understanding of such things.

"Because they are spiritually discerned," and without Christ, one can't have the Holy Spirit, therefore, they can't discern such things.

So, this means a man without God cannot receive anything from the Holy Spirit because to him it is foolishness, neither can he understand them because understanding is given from the Holy Spirit.

Do you have people who mock your faith? You should be able to explain this to your loved ones, especially in your immediate family, so that they are aware that the problem isn't with them, but with the unbeliever who mocks them - and that God is quite well aware of this.

You should make sure your spouse and children know God and all of His majesty, and certainly ensure they are surprised by opposition.

If you suffer abuse for your beliefs, pray. We are and will be persecuted for the name of Jesus Christ, but He can ease the impact of it on us with peace that surpasses understanding, and with understanding itself, by preparing our hearts for the abuses.

It is happening now as it was prophesied in the Bible.

If you're not being persecuted for your beliefs yet, it's coming. At least, it's coming if you're going to be obedient to God and share the good news of salvation with those in need of it. If you are not feeling the heat, that's actually a problem. Get moving by serving. We

can be ineffective and comfortable, displeasing God...
or effective and uncomfortable, knowing this is not our
home and we'll one day be comfortable in Heaven, our
true nation of citizenry.

If you struggle to believe, pray to Jesus to help you
with your unbelief.

It works.

Read God's word.

Don't ever quit or stop, that is exactly what the devil
wants for you, your friends and your family. He wants
you to have no relationship with the One who died for
us and to be tortured in hell for eternity. If you have a
relationship with Christ, the devil wants to interrupt
and hinder that, that you will be ineffective in the work
God has prepared for you to do, missing out on the
blessings of it.

If you're saved, you're sealed for eternity by the
Holy Spirit, and that doesn't change, but if you've only
practiced religion absent a relationship with God, you
will miss the cut.

Don't be the one to whom Jesus says "Depart from
me, for I never knew you."

If you know someone who says they hate reading
(I'm assuming that's not you if you're nearly 200 pages
into this book) download an audio bible onto your
phone. Many of them are free!

The time is now. God is not a vending machine
meant for you to go to only when you find yourself in

need. Do not get stuck in that trap. He is God, worthy of your worship, holy and amazing - yet He is reaching out, hoping for a genuine relationship with you!

It is time to unify our families and educate our children about the Word of God and truth. As parents we will stand before the Lord and we will have to answer for our efforts in teaching our children about faith. Jesus talks very clearly about the consequences of holding our children away from Him or misleading them about Him.

> "But whoever causes one of these little ones who believe in Me to stumble, it would be better for him if a millstone were hung around his neck, and he were thrown into the sea." ~**Mark 9:42**

As parents we are responsible for our children's knowledge and faith in God. It is our duty to supply the knowledge and tools to succeed as a Christian in life and death.

Of course, if you come to faith later in life, and your kids are out on their own, there is grace to cover you not teaching them when they were young about what you yourself didn't know. Now, however, if you have a relationship with your adult children, you should sit them down and tell them of the treasure you've found in Jesus.

But Jesus said, "Let the little children come to Me, and do not forbid them; for of such is the kingdom of heaven." ~**Matthew 19:14**

Train up a child in the way he should go, And when he is old he will not depart from it. ~**Proverbs 22:6**

CHAPTER FORTY

THE POWER OF PRAYER

I have had a strong prayer life, mainly because of my suffering.

Years ago, my nephew invited me to a protestant church. I had never heard modern worship music before and true biblical teachings covering the totality of God's word. It brought my soul into submission, and my heart into joy, and I have never looked back toward the church in which I grew up.

Jesus Christ models praying in the gospels, many times leaving others to pray in solitude, spending time with His Father alone.

Prayer is not meant to be a last-ditch effort. It should be the first and strongest effort for praise and worship, an intimate relationship with Jesus Christ, dealing with life's trials and tribulations and a daily source of guidance for us.

"And when you pray, you shall not be like the hypocrites. For they love to pray standing in the synagogues and on the corners of the streets, that they may be seen by men. Assuredly, I say to you, they have their reward. ⁶ But you, when you pray, go into your room, and when you have shut your door, pray to your Father who *is* in the secret *place;* and your Father who sees in secret will reward you openly. ⁷ And when you pray, do not use vain repetitions as the heathen do. For they think that they will be heard for their many words.

> ⁸ "Therefore do not be like them. For your Father knows the things you have need of before you ask Him. ~**Matthew 6:5-8**

> And He said to them, "It is written, 'My house shall be called a house of prayer,' but you have made it a 'den of thieves.' ~**Matthew 21:13**

> In this manner, therefore, pray:
> Our Father in heaven, Hallowed be Your name. ¹⁰ Your kingdom come.
> Your will be done On earth as *it is* in heaven. ¹¹ Give us this day our daily bread. ¹² And forgive us our debts, As we forgive our debtors. ¹³ And do not lead us into Temptation, But deliver us from the evil one. For Yours is the kingdom and the power and the glory forever. Amen. ~**Matthew 6:9-13**

But I say to you, love your enemies, bless those who curse you, do good to those who hate you, and pray for those who spitefully use you and persecute you, [45] that you may be sons of your Father in heaven; for He makes His sun rise on the evil and on the good, and sends rain on the just and on the unjust. ~**Matthew 5:44-45**

'These people draw near to Me with their mouth, And honor Me with *their* lips,
But their heart is far from Me. [9] And in vain they worship Me, Teaching *as* doctrines the commandments of men.' ~**Matthew 15:8-9**

"AgainI say to you that if two of you agree on earth concerning anything that they ask, it will be done for them by My Father in heaven. [20] For where two or three are gathered together in My name, I am there in the midst of them." ~**Matthew 18:19-20**

So Jesus answered and said to them, "Assuredly, I say to you, if you have faith and do not doubt, you will not only do what was done to the fig tree, but also if you say to this mountain, 'Be removed and be cast into the sea,' it will be done. [22] And whatever things you ask in prayer, believing, you will receive." ~**Matthew 21:21-22**

Watch therefore, and pray always that you may be counted worthy to escape all these things that will come to pass, and to stand before the Son of Man." ~**Luke 21:36**

When He came to the place, He said to them, "Pray that you may not enter into temptation." ~**Luke 22:40**

But the hour is coming, and now is, when the true worshipers will worship the Father in spirit and truth; for the Father is seeking such to worship Him. [24] God *is* Spirit, and those who worship Him must worship in spirit and truth." ~**John 4:23-24**

If you abide in Me, and My words abide in you, you will ask what you desire, and it shall be done for you ~**John 15:7**

"And in that day you will ask Me nothing. Most assuredly, I say to you, whatever you ask the Father in My name He will give you. [24] Until now you have asked nothing in My name. Ask, and you will receive, that your joy may be full. [25] "These things I have spoken to you in figurative language; but the time is coming when I will no longer speak to you in figurative language, but I will tell you plainly about the Father. [26] In that day you will ask in My name, and I do not say to you that I shall pray the Father for you; [27] for the Father Himself loves you, because you have loved Me, and have believed that I came forth from God. ~**John 16:23-27**

CHAPTER FORTY-ONE

SALVATION IN CHRIST

For those of you reading this, I must speak from my heart.

I don't know when the final days are but what God has shown and told me heightens my vigilance that we are getting closer to the final days and the start of end days and times.

I wouldn't be surprised to find that they've already begun and are just getting rolling now. Many of the prophecies have been fulfilled, and many seem to be just on the cusp of happening.

The only reason for this short book is that God commanded me to write it. I'm not a journalist, or a novelist, just a sick old nobody who the Lord has saved physically again and again and for all of eternity.

Jesus tells us it is a narrow path to heaven and few will make it and a wide path to destruction that many will follow.

Hear me. God is. He says of Himself, "I Am." That

means we have to learn who He is because His divine characteristics exist separate from us and without our input. If you have made a god in your mind who fits your own personal preferences, beliefs and/or ideology you are wrong.

God says of Himself that He is not a man that He should change His mind. That means you and I must change in light of his existence and expectations. He can't and won't.

We are to follow His plan for us and live as the bible informs us to throughout the word.

Do you know the Lord's plan for you? If yes, what are you doing about it? If you don't know, go to the Creator in prayer and ask Him.

If you don't hear from Him in that moment, keep asking. He will inform you of His will for you and your life, for He desires for you to live that life.

Are you going to heaven? If you say yes, how do you know it? If you said maybe, why is that? If you said no, but you want to, start today.

Jesus said "I am the Way, the Truth and the Life. No one goes to the Father except through Me."

Do you have a personal relationship with Jesus?

If you don't you will not make it. He will tell His Father that He never knew you. If you truthfully claim you have a relationship with Jesus and have accepted Him as your Savior, you will be saved. In fact, you are.

Those who do not give their lives to Jesus Christ will

not go to Heaven. It's a tough truth for many, and for many people a lot of changes will necessarily have to occur in their lives to live as God wants, just as God had to change my life. Some of it is challenging, and letting go of some things in which you're invested brings about some emotional mourning. However, it will set you free.

If you have never accepted Jesus Christ as your Lord and Savior and you are ready now, pray these words to Jesus with all your heart:

> Jesus, I thank you for dying on the cross for me to erase my sins. I know you were crucified on my behalf, and you rose from the grave three days later, resurrected. You sit at the right hand of the Father, today, intervening on my behalf. Lord, I ask you to forgive my sins and come into my life as my Lord, leading my life and guiding my steps so I may be obedient to You throughout my life here on Earth and one day live with You in eternity, forever and ever.
>
> I ask this in your Holy Name, Jesus Christ Our Savior,
>
> Amen

If you have said these words and totally mean it, with all your heart, you are now a child of God for eternity! Congratulations!

What is Next? After accepting Jesus as your Savior, what do you do?

Turn away from the old life, and turn toward God in all that you learn and do. Sure... but that sound like a tall order. How do I get there??

1. **Read the Bible daily.** It could be a verse or a chapter. Make sure you always understand what is said before moving on. If you don't grasp it, ask someone for help. It is not a race. If you have difficulty reading you can download a free audio app.

2. **Pray, pray, pray.** Everyday. Give thanks and pray for others. Bring your issues and concerns to the Holy Throne of God. You're welcome there, and you're not going to shock him... there is nothing God does not know about you.

3. **Find a church** and have fellowship with other Christians.

4. **Serve.** Find a group or organization (many times within church) that serves the poor, the needy, the

elderly, or the hungry. Help someone learn to read or get a driver's license, teach them to pass their GED test. There is some way God wants to use you to bless others.

5. Share your faith Your story of how God brought you to Him matters and helps those who don't yet know God see that it's not some terrifying or weird thing.

6. Spread the Gospel Your church isn't just for the gathered, but also for the gathering. Lots of people out there are hurting and in need of hope... join in on evangelism efforts to bring that hope to them!

My prayer for you

Dear Jesus Christ my Savior. I thank you for showing and telling me things that I was able to express in this book. I pray that these words have impacted the hearts of readers and helps them thrive in life with you for eternity. Lord, I pray that if any are sick or spiritually troubled, that You fix their bodies and souls to be well, upright, and eternally linked with You.

I pray all of this in your Holy Name, Jesus Christ, The Great I Am.

Amen

CHAPTER FORTY-TWO

MY FRIEND JUDAH

Judah Sills was a young man who showed up at the Good News place while we were serving food and holding a Bible study. He was 24, wearing a 10-gallon cowboy hat, and sporting a smile that could make anyone's day better.

Judah had been abused as a baby and suffered all of his natural life with mental illness due to the damage done. He had a speech impediment, mostly pronouncing his "r's" with the "w" sound, but despite his challenges his heart was gentle and charitable. Gold, really.

I found out much later that once he had been removed from his above birth situation, he'd been blessed by a family who adopted him young, raising him until he was sixteen alongside other adopted children on a rural spread in Oklahoma. He had loving adopted parents and it was clear they were Christian, as Judah had a solid understanding of Jesus and salvation.

On the day he showed up, he was homeless. He

had bounced around hospitals after running away from his people in typical teenage frustration, and for the prior 6 years of his life had been in many towns before wandering into Pittsburgh. That first day, he and I talked for an hour. I could see he was in need, and my spirit was telling me to help him

Working with Judah, he was able to find a job and an apartment, with some agency assistance, and ending up on his feet for the first time in years. His life was turning around. But there were emotional issues, vestiges of trauma he'd suffered young and after he struck out on his own.

During his wandering, Judah had often been beaten up, bouncing between couches, living on the streets, and psych units in hospitals. He was gullible and, in his gentle nature, totally taken advantage of by predatory people over and again.

Innocent and childlike despite the abuses he'd suffered or maybe because of it in some ways, he would trust everyone. And it would bite him sometimes.

He always wanted to help the needy, and began serving with us at Faithbridge, becoming a wonderful church member, loved by all.

When the dark clouds of bad memories came to him, Judah would become depressed, very troubled. His mind would dredge up some trauma, stack on another remembered affront... and he would shut down. He didn't talk much to anyone about his past but me. I would listen, encourage him, and pray with

Him, cajoling him along and reminding him to lean into Jesus when the dark emotions came upon him.

He was lonely for companionship. Married once for a short minute as a teen, he had a great work ethic and labored very hard when he worked, but, due to his challenges most employers only had him do grunt work or filthy labor no one else was willing to suffer quietly. It was important to him that he pleased his bosses and the people he volunteered alongside.

On psych medications, Judah would draw up to the edge of depression when his medicines were running low and he had to ration them. If he crossed the edge, He'd call from a bridge, threatening suicide.

Over time I learned about the misuse and abuse he'd found on the highways. He'd been pummeled dozens of times, often for questioning the ethics of something a group of folks he'd found himself among were doing. He'd been forced to sell drugs as an unpaid slave, pistol whipped, even raped. He'd been ripped off repeatedly.

When I met him, he'd already had $27,000 stolen from an account due to scams and hackers, money he'd gotten from Social Security as a back payment when his disability was approved.

He called countless times from the bridge or as he was heading to it, and I would talk him down. It broke my heart to see him hurting. I knew his heart was amazing and when his head was in a good space, I knew no one kinder, nicer, or more decent to be around... and that made putting up with his bad moments tolerable. I knew that inside that depressed guy was a terrific kid who was struggling.

He was lonely and wanted to marry again, but outside of the nomadic outlaw types he'd found on the road, he didn't know how to find a mate. He tried online dating with his phone, but his gullibility made it a mess.

He'd meet someone online, an avatar picture of a pretty girl claiming to be lonely and interested in him, and believe they loved him and needed help. They would scam him. Several times I would meet Judah at a restaurant where he was waiting for a date that wasn't coming.

He would have two meals and two drinks, one for him and one for the fake girl online who'd promised to meet him there after he sent money.

Time after time he would set meeting places and no one would arrive. He'd be dressed to impress in his best suit, believing that this time the girl was legitimate and would show up. Once he asked for a ride to the airport to pick up the girl he'd wired plane ticket money to, and he showed up dressed to the nines with a dozen roses.

I took him to the airport, trying to prepare him for the let down, but he was positive that she was coming. She'd texted a jpeg of a fight ticket. After we'd climbed back in the car without his dream girl, who, of course, never arrived, I asked for a closer look at the picture of the ticket. It was an old, used boarding pass and the destination was Ft. Lauderdale.

It was heartbreaking, but with his damage, it was hard to get through to him with the truth of the situation because he so longed for a partner, and refused to believe so many people could be so cruel.

I loved Judah like a son. He had needs and I could help, and didn't mind doing so because he was such a nice kid.

And Judah helped me, too. He always prayed for me, worried about me and my health. When I was in the hospital, he would seem lost. We'd talk for hours on the phone as I lay on a hospital bed.

I felt like I was all he had, especially in the area. The others at the church were his friends, but I was more of a surrogate father to him. His adopted brothers and sisters loved and missed him, but they all lived far away and only a couple stayed in regular touch with him. I wished I could do more to help Judah but I was limited by disability, financially and physically.

We were friends for four years. I would drive him to work even though he lived far away from me, and pick him up for church even though he stayed as far to the east of Pittsburgh as I lived to the west. I'd drive past the church, go another 25 minutes, pick him up and head back to the church. We would often go out and eat together. He loved a hamburger special at an IHOP near his place, and we'd eat and talk about his job, his hopes, and he always made sure to ask after me, if I was alright.

His desire for approval wasn't a needy thing, but

a real wish to make others happy. He deserved much more out of life than he got, all along the way.

Judah died at twenty-eight, of myocarditis. He had gotten a Covid-19 vaccine one day, and the caretakers at his building found him dead in bed the next morning.

The four years I had with Judah permanently changed my outlook in my own life. His unconditional love and kindness for me and others was a lesson that I needed to see and learn from.

Judah came into my life like the stranger in the bible, and ended up showing me love and kindness that amazed me, treating me with the decency and love of the Good Samaritan.

He was committed to serving other wandering strangers like himself.

Judah grew in bible study and we could see how God protected him from situations, seeing him through some difficult and dangerous times, allowing Judah to live long enough to solidify his relationship with Jesus and shine for a season before taking him home.

I know Judah is with Jesus and holds a prominent place in heaven with Him. His innocence was childlike, but the maturity of his kindness and love was beyond his years, even after living on the streets and being mistreated while homeless.

I now know Jesus brought Judah to me. We were both in need and it was the plan of Jesus. Praise You Jesus Christ!

My Final Prayer,

Dear Jesus my loving Savior,

Thank You for watching over me while writing this, Lord. Please use it for Your glory. I pray that those who read this are moved by Your love and saving grace and are transformed. That they would see Your powerful Spirit at work and learn to go deeper with Him. Help the readers not just read this book, but love Your holy word, so they can be transformed by the renewing of their minds to live a lives of obedience and truth for You. Lord, have mercy upon those who suffer physically and or spiritually when they call upon Your mighty name for relief and healing. Touch and show them Your love for them and Your desire to know them for eternity. Help me carry a stamp upon my heart with the love for the stranger that I got to see and experience in my friend Judah.

And, if it's OK with You, Lord... give him a big hug for me.

I pray and ask all of this in the Holiest name above all names,

Jesus Christ

Amen

Printed in the United States
by Baker & Taylor Publisher Services